LA

ANTISEMITISM

HERMANN BAHR

ANTISEMITISM

*Translated from the German and
with an afterword by James J. Conway*

RIXDORF EDITIONS BERLIN 2019

Antisemitism by Hermann Bahr was first published in German as
Der Antisemitismus. Ein internationales Interview by S. Fischer, Verlag in
Berlin, 1894. With the exception of the interview with Henri Rochefort, the
constituent parts were first published in the *Deutsche Zeitung*, Vienna,
in the series *Der Antisemitismus. Ein internationales Interview*, which ran
from March to September 1893.

This translation and afterword © 2019 James J. Conway

Antisemitism
first published Rixdorf Editions, Berlin, 2019

Design by Svenja Prigge; front-cover image from an undated postcard of
Édouard Drumont by Philippe Norwins

Printed by Totem.com.pl, Inowrocław, Poland

ISBN: 978-3-947325-10-8

All rights reserved. No part of this publication may be reproduced, stored
in a retrieval system, or transmitted, in any form or by any means, without
the prior written permission of Rixdorf Editions, except for legitimate
review purposes.

RixdorfEditions.com

CONTENTS

ANTISEMITISM

To my dear friend
Imperial Councillor
Dr Emil Auspitzer[1]
Vienna, September 1893

AUTHOR'S INTRODUCTION[2]

Once again I am venturing out into the world to find out what people are thinking and saying. This time I wish to question them about antisemitism. Not to gather reasons for or against it, which are tawdry and ineffectual; but rather to gather a few credible documents in these confused times – without anger, without love – that show how the educated among the different peoples, the different nations really think about this matter today.

There are many books on the subject. Some are clever, others foolish, but none of them hit the mark. They are muddled, acting as though it were a question of reasons, or proof. But I believe there is something else occurring here. I have my own particular opinion on the matter; I would not force it on anyone, but perhaps I may share it with you.

Antisemitism desires only itself. It is not, for instance, a means to an end. The sole purpose of anti-semitism is antisemitism. One is an antisemite for the sake of being an antisemite. One wallows in the sensation.

It is a function of the times in which we live that people desire artificial stimulants to gather their withered, ravaged nerves. They serve as a replacement for the tender intoxication the masses once found in forgotten faith and vanished ideals. The rich reach for their morphine and hashish. Those who cannot afford them become antisemites. Antisemitism is the morphine of the little people.

It is the desire for passion, verve and delirium, and the natural sources of these things are exhausted. There are no great ideas, no moral pathos which might arouse the delights of rapture. And for lack of sensual love, one turns to sensual hatred. One need only taste it once with one's own senses and nerves to know its seductive poison. The object of the hatred is essentially neither here nor there. The Jew is simply convenient. For the same purpose the French began by using the Prussian, and then the Jew, and lately the banker, and for them it was never a matter of the Prussian or the Jew or the banker; it was always a matter of the hatred, and the mighty excitement it supplies. If there were no Jews, antisemites would have to invent them. Otherwise they would be deprived of the pleasure this powerful excitation offers them.

This, I believe, is the psychology of antisemitism among the masses. For the 'leaders' there is most likely something else at stake. For the demagogue there is no more convenient instrument.

I was once chatting with Maurice Barrès[3], who was enthusing about Rochefort[4]. I had to laugh about the curious alliance of the Wagner admirer and the anti-*Lohengrin* agitator. But he defended his friend. 'Believe me, he values the dignity and the worth of Wagner as much as you or I; yet he would struggle to find anything more apt with which to seize the masses – if you wish for mastery over the masses you cannot afford to let an opportunity for passion pass you by.'

Those antisemitic leaders who are not solely concerned with business are claimants to the favour of the mob that they wish to rule. In their limited circle they aspire to be the Nietzschean *Übermensch* who attains the pleasure of power by any means necessary. It titillates them to play upon the instincts and desires of the masses as if they were a keyboard that responds to the slightest pressure.

This is what I think about antisemitism and why I believe that one cannot use arguments against it. Antisemites are antisemites out of desire for the delirium and intoxication of passion. They seize the arguments that are closest to hand. Should you debunk them, they will seek others. And if they should find none it will not change their minds. They do not wish to forgo the intoxication. Nought but a nobler delirium will cure them, when the masses are given another ideal, a moral pathos. It is for this reason that socialism may well be the sole physician of antisemitism.

So I do not at all intend to 'refute' antisemitism, which has been refuted a thousand times to no avail. I simply ask: what impressions do the educated of the various nations have of this phenomenon among the populace, and how do they respond? Perhaps at a later date this will result in a wholly curious document of the state of mind around 1893.

FRIEDRICH SPIELHAGEN

Hohenzollernstrasse[5], wide, white and empty, leads to the long, long street that borders the Tiergarten. Your footsteps echo and there is not a human sound to be heard. Only on the corner is there a shrivelled, scrawny woman selling wilting yellow stalks as though they were actual flowers.

Each building like the next, stiff and austere; all so correct. Each has a little narrow yard and railing in front. They will put a tree out there in summer, a few roses, and proudly remark how pretty it is, how every little house has its own garden here, something you rarely find in Vienna.

The second floor. I am led into a chamber which is a blend of good room, salon and atelier. There is a bourgeois sobriety to its plain, pedantic order – but also a lady's chaise longues and causeuses – with a nobler grace to the busts and paintings. It resembles the home of a well-placed provincial bourgeois with a dull job who yet elects to cultivate beauty in his idle hours – a serene mind that may at times toy with the emotions, in moderation and wisdom. Diligence must feel at home here; certainly there is nothing to satisfy the finer sensibility that lusts after exquisite sensations.

Taut and tight, clipped and alert, straight and sharp is his manner. One might take him for a high-ranking officer or a Prussian judge whose limbs retain the training of his 'corps'; every gesture attests to a youth spent in discipline. I am surprised to find so much of the soldier, even the policeman in this brave warrior for liberty. The gentle, positively sentimental nature of his books belies his true character. He is highly hospitable, yet even in his courtesy there is measure and rigour, much like a second negotiating with the referee at a duel – with great respect, but retaining something of his combative metier.

A hard, rigid profile. He resembles a swift sketch that seeks only to record the characteristic features, eschewing all that is indecisive or mutable. His hair and the narrow beard around his cracked lips are kept short. With the last of the day slowly expiring, I am unable to judge in the darkness whether it is grey or light brown. There is nothing of the poet in the sober, clever gaze behind the pince-nez; he is more akin to a prosecutor or inquisitor looking for clues. His concise speech lacks the circuitousness of his writing; he speaks in clipped haste, rapidly issuing contingent sets of words, yet pausing abruptly between phrases as a new thought begins, as though he first wished to reflect on the logical order – it is not so much chatter as dictation.

'I do not know, sir, if you still remember me – years ago I had '

'But of course – from the Literary Society[6]! We are old acquaintances.'

We take our seats. He offers cigarettes. And I present my request, that he might tell me what he thinks about antisemitism.

'Gladly. But I am afraid it shall be of little use. Reasons, arguments and any kind of moral indignation are powerless against it. It has been attempted many times, and it has never worked. It cannot be approached from this – as I would put it – psychological perspective. One must approach it from the economic perspective. It is an economic question and it calls for an economic solution. As long as we fail to support the economically weak in the struggle against the economically strong, as long as the little man is mercilessly exposed to economic forces, as long as the shameful usury I witnessed in Thuringia is allowed to prevail (and I hear tell of similar things in Baden and Württemberg), any form of education or intellectual culture is powerless against antisemitism. The unspeakable misery that the usurers in rural areas …'

'But surely there are Christian usurers as well …'

'No doubt, but let us not fool ourselves – they are generally Jewish. Perhaps it is their talent that makes Jews economically superior, perhaps it is because they are unscrupulous enough to exploit this superiority – that is not for me to judge. But it is here, in economic distress, that the root of antisemitism lies, and it is here, with the strengthening and recovery of the economically weak and outcast, that the healing must begin. It is a purely economic phenomenon. Anything religious or nationalistic in it is merely mask and pretext.'

'That is more or less what the socialists say, too ...'

'So call me a socialist if you wish. I shall not object. The more I reflect on humanity and the future of my people, the more conscious and sure I am – even though I do not profess to be of the party that bears this name, most likely cannot profess, because to the necessity and inevitability of economic reform they conjoin all manner of vapid, utopian quirks which merely cause confusion. But that blithe, merry Manchesterism[7] is finished, never to return. It was perhaps Bismarck's greatest deed that he recognised this and pointed to a new path, even if his strength, perhaps his entire manner were not sufficient for him to attain its end. And when you think of pensions, disability insurance and such[8], is socialism not already in our midst? If we simply let it be and pursue this new path with vigour, soon you will find no trace of antisemitism. It must be resolved through economics, for it is a purely economic issue.'

'But there is antisemitism that has nothing to do with the economy – among students, for example. One cannot claim that the Jewish student is wealthier ...'

'Not wealthier, but superior in competition and a financial danger to our idle, slow youth. The Jewish student arrives at lectures on time, takes the best seat and has long been busily taking notes when the sullen German finally drags himself in with yesterday's hangover still weighing down his limbs, forced to sit in the inferior seats and barely able to follow the lecture. Punishment comes with the exams, where the Jew knows more, and gets the better marks – and punishment comes in life, where the Jew is mentally equipped for every eventuality.'

'You almost sound like the antisemites who portray the Jews as superior in intelligence and diligence to the Teutons – which flatters the Jews greatly, but according to my experience is not at all true.'

'Diligence, absolutely – they are certainly superior in diligence. And in certain intellectual gifts. But it does not suffice for the truly great things. The average intelligence of the Jews is decidedly higher than the average intelligence of the Teutons. But they have signally failed to attain the apex of the sciences, the arts.'

'Heinrich Heine[9] …'

'Naturally Heine is a peak of our literature, but one that is dwarfed by summits such as Goethe and Schiller. That is precisely what I was just saying.'

'Spinoza[10] –'

'I am such a thorough-going devotee of Spinoza, in every sensation and thought, that the name alone affords me the deepest sense of awe. But an exception merely confirms the rule.'

THEODOR BARTH

From the Brandenburg Gate I cross the Tiergarten, past the loud, impudent column with the outsized Viktoria[11], known as the purest girl in Berlin because no man can measure up to her. Over there to the left is the long, long street[12] they are so proud of here, with the garish embellishments adorning every building alerting you to the many millions dwelling inside. His home is at the very end, the last of the long, long street.

The Free-Minded Party[13] value Theodor Barth highly because he is one of those working parliamentarians who are becoming increasingly rare. You might not often see him at the podium, but the committees are familiar with his diligence. He has elected to undertake the thankless work that fêted orators would sooner avoid – the hard graft of political business. They praise his inexhaustible strength, always at the ready. The people of Bremen rhapsodise still about the erstwhile secretary of their chamber of commerce[14], and his thoughtful care and resourceful zeal have made the *Nation*[15], which he now leads for the tenth year, the darling of bourgeois taste.

He is short, unprepossessing, and his narrow blond beard frames tired, drained, almost pained features. They appear soft, wavering and changeable, and only when his conversation reaches a point of agitation do they assume a comprehensible resolve. Behind his glasses, beneath reddened lids he has the groping gaze of the short-sighted – I am reminded of Jules Lemaître[16]. He speaks questingly, haltingly, often inserting a thought between others, shuffling sentences together, and he tends to finish his words with a hesitant gesture that he soon indecisively abandons, a soft smile, a half-question. It is not so much conversation, or even talking, as thinking aloud.

'Antisemitism is a kind of socialism of the Junkers … by the Junkers and for the Junkers. Anything nationalist or religious in it is merely a cover, a pretext. The lesser Junkers are consigned to ruin, condemned to destruction by modern development. They cannot reconcile themselves to the momentum of economic development, their decline is inexorable. Naturally they will not go quietly, rather they will defend themselves to the best of their ability, which, however, will not help at all because the force of this economic process is irresistible, insurmountable. Hence their hatred of a development that promises their extinction – and the most tangible expression of this development is the Jew. Hence their fierce desire to inhibit it at any price, to forcefully stall it by making the power of the state mistrustful of it and trying to draw it back to the past – and the best means of deterring state power from development is once again the Jew, agitation against the Jew. It is quite natural that they should hate Jews because the Jews more or less symbolise the hated era that signals their end. Fomenting against the Jews serves their purposes admirably, because it is only uproar and turmoil among the mob that will alarm the forces of the state and thwart natural development. In the end they may actually succeed, continuing a little further at the expense of others, as the power of the state allows them to enrich themselves from others – their levies, their alms, the tax plans of Mr Miquel[17], the whole issue of bimetallism[18] that they see as a simple reduction of all debts at the cost of creditors, as an official Seisachtheia[19], all their 'reforms' aim at nothing more than provisioning them from the pockets of others. They mean for anti-semitism to assist in this by making the state question modern development, so that it becomes discouraged and frightened and places its power at their service once more. They are the true Catilinarians[20] who require uproar, noise and embitterment so that they might fish in troubled waters. They care not a jot if they should disturb the peace of the land, or even imperil the realm that they so readily invoke. All they ever want is their own advantage. They need confusion, dissatisfaction and the appearance of increasing indignation among the masses. That is why they are stirring up the worst elements – deprived workers, unemployed civil servants, the déclassé of every stripe, shadowy individuals –'

'What Marx called the *Lumpenproletariat* –'

'Yes – they are their instruments. And they are led by professional demagogues like Ahlwardt[21]. Bismarck is also to blame; because it was the unbridled frivolity and cynical innocuousness of his policies that allowed such people to rise in the first place. A man who is found guilty of slander in every trial – and with every trial the power and the zeal of his party only grows! It has now been proven that there is nothing, absolutely nothing, not an iota, not a shadow of truth in any of his claims or complaints – and all the while the man seems so pleased with himself, laughing at us all, greeted on the street with enthusiasm and jubilation the likes of which even Bismarck only witnessed at the zenith of his most exuberant popularity.'

'What manner of man is he actually – psychologically I mean?'

'I cannot rightly say – perhaps a fanatic, certainly a speculator, the two jumbled together in some strange way, probably a sick individual. Sometimes he seems positively possessed of an *idée fixe*, and the ridiculous delusion of his mission ...'

'An orator?'

'Not a trace. He babbles vapidly, a thousand ridiculous things all mixed up together – you cannot even tell what he wants. It is simply a mystery what the masses find in him – except the mean pleasure of slander, defamation and scandal; the mob seeks amusement, and nothing amuses it more than hearing decent people slandered and insulted. Lately we have witnessed inadvisable efforts to prosecute him – and so the mob have come to regard him as a genuine martyr and a hero. And in the face of that, any form of reason is defenceless, futile.'

'But what do you think will come of it? It cannot continue like this!'

'Yes … that is hard to say. Under normal conditions there would be no danger. We have contended with worse in the past. But now we have this hopeless political situation which is more foolishly complicated than ever. Just think! In the interests of prosperous development we could not wish for a better minister than Caprivi[22]; the Junkers cannot imagine anyone worse. We have every reason to retain him; they have every reason to bring him down. But now, with the Army Bill[23], we are compelled by the electorate to vote against the one whose fall no one would lament more than us; and the Junkers are forced to vote in favour of the one whose fall no one wishes more fervently than they. It would be our worst defeat if we should win now, and their greatest victory if they lose. And to extend this absurdity even further – for us it is not even about the principle. A few thousand soldiers more or less – in the end it is only a matter of proportion, not of principle. We could easily make real concessions without abandoning the programme in the least. But we are not allowed to because our voters do not wish it – and ultimately it is the voters who are paying for the whole thing. We cannot dispose of their money against their will. That is why we will probably cause a minister to fall whose preservation is in our greatest interest, to the greatest joy of the Conservatives who seem to defend him against us and yet certainly cannot wait for his downfall.'

'That is actually highly amusing –'

'Yes, it may be amusing if it does not concern you. For us it is very sad, and nobody knows what to do about it. And ultimately one should not be surprised if the finest and noblest of the nation are turning away from politics in disgust. It has reached the point now that we only stand for office out of shame and obligation, and we envy those who are voted out. Everything is spoiled, and many stalwart champions of liberty are already lamenting universal suffrage.'

'Strange – when I was last in Paris the French often told me the same thing.'

'It appears to be international; for decent people politics is denatured, and it is increasingly becoming a business of speculators. Of course, they could not wish for anything better than the current circumstances. Their stock is high. The *Staatsbürger-Zeitung*[24] has gained three thousand subscribers in the last quarter with anti-semitic agitation, and in this quarter it may gain even more. If you simply cater to the lowest instincts without conscience – these are the only people who are satisfied with politics right now.'

'You take a dark view …'

'We have every reason to. Wherever we look the future seems murky, and there is only one hope: the workers, and socialism. In the struggle against antisemitism, socialism has revealed itself first of all as a factor of German culture by resisting all temptations and remaining true to us. And if you wish to regain a measure of confidence and reliability you have to look to socialism. The socialists are the most dependable guardians of freedom, the most honest servants of healthy development –'

'Well – from the point of view of capitalist interests –?'

'Oh … because of certain economic utopias?

They are receding more and more and have become quite platonic over time. They do not deny them, but they are of almost no significance. It is like a pious belief in a better life after death – little more than that. You can let them have it and I believe it was a major tactical mistake when Richter[25] recently spoke against them. There is absolutely no point. In every political question it is only the Social Democrats who are our natural allies today, and I do not doubt that they will refine even more over time and turn into a radical workers' party, and fight shoulder to shoulder with us. We can only fervently wish that next time 72 enter the house instead of the 36 that they are now, and it goes without saying that between Conservatives and Social Democrats we will always choose the Social Democrats. Because it is only with their help that we will finally manage to successfully overcome and subdue these vile and adverse circumstances.'

AUGUST BEBEL

Way out on Grossgörschenstrasse[26], where the remains of the city expire; the buildings are further apart, the paltry vegetation sways, and the empty countryside peers in.

A narrow, quiet, bright room. Books and papers, simple engravings and woodcuts of democrats and socialists on the plain wall, the leonine head of Marx triumphing over them all; yet more papers and books. A happy, tranquil, gentle atmosphere of untroubled, devoted labour.

His head is often compared to that of Christ. But this is a Saxon Christ – soft, shy, almost a little prim. You see the same tired, sad features in Ola Hansson's[27] women, an exhaustion and pallor caused less by great turns of fate than small daily sorrows.

He greets me with his calm, solemn cordiality. It was in Paris that we last saw each other, in 1889, at the Socialist Congress[28]. But he is not altogether delighted when I tell him why I have come today.

ANTISEMITISM

'One does not always have the best experience with interviews. Things are easily misinterpreted, and yet one cannot always rectify them straight away. And so newspapers print a good deal of things that are not true, which is vexing. I do not know if you heard the serious proposal that was presented to us at the last congress about this – it was to do with French journalists; there was no formal decision, but the sentiment was that in future we should steer clear of such things.'

But gradually he eases into conversation. He has a simple, thoughtful way of bringing forth words with his head cocked a little. It is more like a monologue to himself, one which I do not wish to disturb.

'One of your countrymen – I believe it was Kronawetter – once said, 'antisemitism is the socialism of fools.'[29] That is a nice formulation, but it does not get to the heart of the matter. The true adherents of anti-semitism, the small traders and the small landowners, are not entirely wrong from their point of view. It is largely in the figure of the Jew that they encounter capital. In Hesse and other parts of south-western Germany, for example – where I am familiar with conditions – mort-gages are in the hands of the Jews and in every market the buyers of agricultural products are Jews. As a result, the negative effects of capitalism always appear in the guise of the Jew, and of course it is natural that these classes, who are not given to pondering the capitalist system at length, but rather abide by the forms and experiences in which it confronts them, succumb to antisemitism. Small businesses are in turn greatly affected by com-petition from Jewish traders, with clothes stores, shoe stores, manufactured goods stores and so on almost exclusively in the hands of the Jews, and their competition is overwhelming for these classes. Officers and civil servants have other reasons. Many of them have debts and once again the creditor is very often a Jew – hence their hatred of them. Meanwhile the students do not like Jews partly because they are also often in debt to them, but also because Jewish students are often more diligent and, as a race, probably more intelligent. So more or less everything depends on economic conditions. Things are different in the East, where the Jews are poor and often workers, or farmers. The Jews who come to us are usually a more select element, the more intelligent, who have a better chance in competition. And then there is the national aspect – which you do not find in the Romance countries; the Spaniards and Italians are far more intermixed with the Jews and often cannot distinguish the Jews from their own nationality. The Germans readily recognise the Jew and therefore regard him as a foreigner, and among the less intellectual element in particular, race is always of great import. So one is perfectly able to explain antisemitism from factual circumstances, and then comes the fact of it being artificially promoted and stoked by all sorts of people.'

'Yes, that would explain antisemitism, but it does not explain the spell that people such as Ahlwardt cast over the mob, with words that are proven to be slander …'

'Ahlwardt only exerts influence because he feels and thinks in the same way as the class of people who follow him. For his followers it is enough if only some of his accusations are true. And you cannot even say that they are wrong, for there is always an element of truth to his stories. There is even some truth in the 'Jew Guns'[30] story; it has been proven in court that there were irregularities – as there are everywhere; anyone who has been a worker or an employer will know that. For example, I used to make door handles, and I know that sometimes a worker will bungle the hole and then simply cover it up. So Ahlwardt was not lying about the irregularities, but he exaggerated them a great deal; and they have nothing to do with Loewe[31], who was not responsible for the technical side. This is what generally happens with Ahlwardt; he will target a particular person with his revelations but strike someone else completely. And it is happening again. He has not proven anything yet, but it is certainly possible that there is some truth to these stories. But ultimately it may not be a Jew he strikes but Miquel[32], the darling of the Conservatives, whom they would most like to see as Chancellor. And that is how it always is with him. He is a confused individual who is unaware of the impact of his actions. One can only feel sorry for him, as Lieber[33] rightly said yesterday. He talks nonsense, it is all muddled. What the newspapers report about his speeches strikes me as far too favourable. When he speaks, the sentences disappear, but still they express something amid a murky mess of phrases. That is why the 'German Panama'[34], as they are calling it, will end quietly. The documents to which he has access are not in the hands of someone who could do something with them. And on top of that the stories are old; we know them from Otto Glagau, Rudolf Meyer, from the *Reichsglocke*[35]. But in possessing the files he offers the impression that he can prove things that others only claim. He makes mention, for example, of a letter from a Romanian president to Miquel, who tore it up and threw it in the bin, which a servant fished out and stuck together. In it the President is said to have acknowledged the receipt of a sum which Ahlwardt considers to be a bribe[36]. It also concerns the Hanover-Altenbekener Railway[37], shares in which were artificially increased prior to nationalisation. For all this he claims to have all sorts of documents. Whether he knows what to do with them is another question. He gets bogged down. To date he has not been able to prove anything that he has brought forth. But these claims still have an effect on his people. They believe there is something to them. It can only serve our purposes if the ruling classes should fight each other, if confidence wanes and disgust at this order of society grows. We shall watch and wait.'

THEODOR MOMMSEN

Out in Charlottenburg, hidden behind bright gardens. There you find Marchstrasse dreaming quietly with little more accompaniment than the occasional gentle tolling of the horse tram bell[38]. There you find his ponderous little house, shying away from the others, leaning sideways a little.

I am led into a small sitting room. Heavy, sober, dark furniture; mild, deep colours; not a trace of frippery. You are confronted by the same solemn joy that you feel on entering Count Schack's gallery[39]. A beautiful full copy of a Titian and etchings of the finest wonders of the Italians all around, from the lean nobility of the Pre-Raphaelites onwards; Leonardo's wise, whimsical, drily seductive women and the mature grace of Titian's Bella. Beauty undergoes transformation here, from first desire to the most prodigious fulfilment.

He is bowed by old age, and as he trudges, a little awkward and stiff, with an elaborate courtesy now fallen from fashion, a sheepish, perplexed kindness in his hesitant gestures, he presents an inexpressibly touching spectacle. His sunken form is swamped by a deep, black coat with wide bulging folds, his frail head immersed in the bright glow cast by a light wreath of white curls. A skull that makes you think of Voltaire, with a long, sharp, pointed nose and wan, faded cheeks which appear to be carved in bronze, with thin, pale, constantly moving lips that appear to be on the lookout for mocking cruelty. This withered, crooked, wrinkled, grave, dishevelled little man might well bring to mind an Oberländer professor from the *Fliegende Blätter*[40], and it almost makes one smile. But when he raises his head and casts his eyes at his guest, those blue eyes behind his narrow golden spectacles cast such a spell of power and goodness that one must bow one's head.

He takes his seat and remains stiff and motionless as he talks. Only his long, narrow, shrunken fingers are in motion, now pressed to his forehead, now passing over his long strands of hair, at times pushed under his brittle chin, shaky gestures constantly straying over a body that does not stir. He speaks very softly, with a slight hiss, and he has a strange way of clicking his lips and wiping them with his tongue after every few words.

I present my request, and explain why we trust his word, and believe that it will have an effect, that it will help and purify. He smiles sadly. 'If you believe I can do anything about it, you are mistaken. If you believe that reason can achieve anything here, you are mistaken. I once believed that as well, and again and again I protested the monstrous shame known as antisemitism. But it does no good. It is completely useless. Anything I could tell you, anything one can say on the matter would only ever be reasons, logical and moral arguments. No antisemite will listen to that. They only listen to their own hatred and their own envy, to their most shameful instincts. They do not care about anything else. They are deaf to reason, law and custom. One cannot affect them. And what could one say to those who follow the 'Headmaster of All Germans'[41]? They cannot be saved. There is no protection against the mob – whether it is the mob on the street or the mob in the salon, it makes no difference; a scoundrel is a scoundrel, and antisemitism is the creed of the scoundrel. It is like a ghastly epidemic, like cholera – it can neither be explained nor cured. You must wait patiently until the poison has run its course and lost its power. And that cannot be far off now. The plague must finally exhaust itself, and it surely cannot go further than Ahlwardt. Perhaps the turning point to gradual recovery, liberation and healing is slowly approaching. Perhaps the delusion that has bewitched so many minds and set our whole culture back a hundred years is vanishing. But any reasons, the finest arguments are in vain. Anyone who is accessible to reason and argumentation cannot even be an antisemite. But those who follow nothing but their wild hatred in defiance of education, liberty and humanity cannot be converted by evidence. Antisemitism cannot be refuted any more than a disease can be refuted. One must wait patiently until the fundamentally healthy nature of the people stirs once again and casts the rot off itself. Of course, you may accelerate and promote recovery by lending it the support of moral forces. And for a long time now I have had an idea that strikes me as more effective than your *enquête*. What can I tell you about antisemitism that is new? And if there were something, what good would it do? All the means of reason are ineffective here, but the weight of renowned personages, of authority may work. People do not listen to individuals at all, but an international declaration could compel respect. *If you were to compose a brief protest against antisemitism, repeating the known reasons in a few sentences, and if it were signed by all the great men of Europe,* whether from science or the arts or politics, *the intellectual nobility of all countries and peoples* – that, I think, could not fail to have an effect[42]. I would take part with great enthusiasm. And you, as an Austrian, could well successfully initiate it, *for you are fortunate enough to possess an unspoiled aristocracy of conviction and morals which is worthy of the name and which honours its traditions, and has bravely resisted all the temptations of antisemitism, and did not hesitate to fight for freedom in the first encounter of the great battle.* You could gain for this protest a few good names who have enjoyed unbroken fame for centuries. Perhaps ultimately that may bring some to their senses, and at least we would salvage our honour in the eyes our grandchildren, if we were to leave them a document that showed the good men of all nations in league against this shameful disease of our time.'

GUSTAV SCHMOLLER

Seated before him once more, this man who was once my teacher, sitting in the large, wide library of his little house, I am reminded of the words of Marx: 'The petty bourgeoisie is made up of on-the-one-hand and on-the-other-hand.' That was a joke we often applied to him at the time, and we were glad of the care and caution with which he managed to turn and interpret everything, until pro and contra were in balance every time and the decision had to be postponed a little because the question was apparently not yet mature. And so we learned a great deal from the master of economics until finally we knew nothing at all.

His 'historical method' was in existence before him. I believe Hildebrand[43] to be the father of it in Germany, and once we abandoned the stiff algebra of the British economists, it duly thrived. But he became the first virtuoso of the new doctrine of political utility by using the most sensitive problems of the day to prove – and this recommended it to every faction – that it is an advocate for any question, providing an equal counter-argument to everyone one of its arguments. This is extremely useful, as the immutable laws of the precise dogmatists always induce a measure of chagrin. Historically, one may decide as one sees fit at the time without being bound for the future – because time always bring new documents, trade regulations, city charters that cast a new light on things.

Anyone in the state who wished to advance, to ascend, went to him, and he became the fêted teacher. Anyone who was already ascendant in the state valued his ever-useful opinion, and he became a State Councillor. The 'historical method' has proven its worth.

And now, years later, he sits before me again, just as he did then, in the soft, loose, billowing clothes which lend him an American nonchalance, with his slow, mild speech gliding as though slipper-shod, with the homely, broad Swabian hiss of his tongue, with his stern expression creased by diligence and effort, continually undermined by the mocking play of his tiny, nimble and wickedly amused eyes – there is mischief afoot in those subtle, warm, chestnut eyes, impudently offering the most wondrous commentary on the solemn sentences that the State Councillor delivers with deliberation, irreverently plucking the white beard of scholarship.

He is not particularly pleased with my request and remains ponderously silent for some time. Then slowly he raises his head a little, which he cocks to hear, beholds me with a smirk and, to cover the mockery of his fine lips, strokes his long white beard, which he twists and puts in his mouth, lost in thought, and there is a twinkling in those wise starlets, as if he did not wish to disturb the peace after all, and he begins. He starts each sentence with 'maybe'; instead of 'not' he says 'hardly', and one must not forget 'approximately'. And if he does forget it on occasion, you hear it in his tone of voice nonetheless.

'I can scarcely tell you anything new – you will find my position on the Jewish question in my essay on Lasker (*On Social and Commercial Law of the Present Day*)[44]; most likely I will soon issue a public pronouncement on the question of different races living together. There has been far too little research or discussion to allow a definitive judgment on the question of whether there are advantages or only certain disadvantages and dangers when a state is composed of different races, when they live among each other, are free to interact and mix. I little doubt that dwelling among one another, mixing, and cross-breeding of races that are physically, mentally, and morally very different from each other brings grave peril to the state and the culture. It is to this that Hehn[45] traces the decline of Rome in the centuries of the imperial period; for this reason, the older Indian civilisations have the harshest prohibitions on connubium, the strictest separation of the races. But as for the Jews, there are two things we must examine: 1. whether there is too great a number of them to digest and assimilate, and 2. whether Teutons and Semites really do differ to such an extent that mixing would be disadvantageous. With a modest influx and a lesser degree of difference, the mixture may even offer great advantages, and the Jews certainly have a number of qualities whose inclusion in the national character, customs, and habits of the Indo-Germans would appear desirable. But theoretically, it must be noted that under certain circumstances a race and its culture may be seriously threatened by excessive admixture of foreign racial elements, and that it is then the state's duty to devise measures for preventing this. Without doubt Coolies, Chinese, Negroes and other races that are far too alien, too different from our own physical and moral habitus must not be permitted, and certainly not in great number, and so one may well plead for a restriction of immigration from the East, not only of the eastern Jews coming from Poland and Russia – who may in fact be Tartars rather than Semites – but also of the invasion of Slavic farm labourers whose standard of living is so much lower than ours.

As far as emancipation of the Jews is concerned, I am of the opinion that people with a moral code too distinct from our own should never be admitted as equal citizens. In approving of equality for the Jews, I do so not because I attribute a right to everything that has a human countenance[46], but because I believe that the fundamental moral teachings of the rabbis and Christian pastors today are influenced by the philosophy of the 18th century and are really much the same, or similar. Naturally this equality cannot be repealed in our civilised central and western European states today. One must merely seek to promote the assimilation of the various racial elements through unitary education and by strengthening the unitary elements in customs and morals. The process of assimilation aims at upholding outer propriety and harmony, not agitating for it, and we should treat the good elements of Judaism as good, the bad ones as bad – that is, treat each as an individual, not as an estate or class. I have always endeavoured to treat the decent, talented Jew as a full equal, to promote him where this was justified, to encourage, but also to dismiss the worst elements, chiefly those that distinguish themselves solely through a certain ingenuity, cleverness, agility and impudence. The assimilation process is aggravated by the sensitivity of the Jews, who all feel solidarity with each other, and should one touch on a wickedness committed by an individual Jew, they all feel affected. This impedes unbiased discussion of the issue, which is also alloyed with certain social and economic factors. Our *haute finance* and stock markets are almost entirely Jewish, so too the small rural lenders, the cattle traders and cattle agents, and in these circles there is impropriety and theft which you as an erstwhile Social Democrat must know and admit.'

'It is just that I do not hold the Aryan capitalist to be somehow more sympathetic than the Semitic.'

'Perhaps he is – or at least he appears more sympathetic to the Aryan worker, because he always retains a certain feeling of kinship for them which the Jew lacks, and therefore he is more inclined to proceed with greater care, with less severity. That must also be considered. But the crucial thing remains the question of race, which could well afford more thorough investigation and exploration than it has enjoyed to date.'

PASTOR J. SCHMEIDLER

I am waiting in a narrow, quiet room decked in diffident grey shades and offering meagre comfort. A desk, a sofa, an armchair, cabinets, a large bust of Luther, small ones of Goethe and Schiller, a glass box with butterflies and beetles. I am waiting some time, and I hear an exchange between two voices in the next room but I cannot make out what they are saying; one timid and perplexed voice enquiring, another deep, soft, mild voice consoling and assisting. Outside, the doorbell rings frequently. It is just before Easter, a time of mounting worries for the preacher who is venerated by the children of his parish with sincere love and regarded rather like a simple saint, ready with advice and encouragement for the soul's every distress.

The pitiful, encumbered, questing voice departs. I enter a large, wide room with numerous books and papers on desks and stands, and above them austere, solemn engravings which exude piety and beauty. The pastor is grave and gentle. His sharp, Dante-esque features are transfigured by a quiet goodness, his white beard and white curls a bright glowing frame for his gentle, serene expression. I present my request and he wishes to fulfil it. He is always ready to work on behalf of peace, reconciliation. Only now, pressed by paschal duties as he is he cannot listen or talk to me, and he would rather send me a few lines that clearly express his opinion.

He then sent me this letter:

Berlin, 4 April 1893.

Dear Sir!

In reply to your request that I characterise my position on antisemitism in a few sentences, I can only assert that I have never, either from a Christian or national point of view, found cause to oppose the Jews as such, and that I can only regard the formation of a political party with that aim as an aberration, behind which I suspect other causes may lie. As a Christian, I know only good and evil, as a citizen only legal and illegal. On the assertion that certain forms of evil in the life of the society are associated with Judaism as such, to date I have detected nothing in them but the improper transference of individual observations to the whole, but if this assertion were better justified than it has been to date I would demand historical consideration that would at the same time provide means of counteraction other than antisemitism. A strict examination of any defects that may lie in Judaism is something I expect and demand above all from Judaism itself.

This is my general position on the matter which to date has only been confirmed by my personal experience in many forms of contact with Jews and especially with the numerous proselytes whose conversion I have only ever mediated after prolonged exchange.

Respectfully yours,
Sincerely,

Schmeidler, preacher.

MAXIMILIAN HARDEN

Born in 1861; in 1881 a minor actor with neither luck nor prospects; in 1890 a reviewer for the weekly journals, where he first attracted the attention of the cognoscenti; in 1891 the abhorred mocker of Berlin; in 1892 the only German journalist in the European style; in 1893 friend of the great Chancellor and victor in the trial concerning the 'education' of the monarch[47]. Quite a fine career. So it is probably worth hearing from this man, speaking to this man and explaining his transformations, his development.

When I came to Berlin in 1890, it was an odd place. Loudly and avidly they argued for and against the 'new art', and fierce attempts to revive poetry, drama and the novel found success. But this youthful impetus neglected criticism, which failed to advance, and remained undisturbed in its rigid forms; for some this was patriarchal, devoid of meaning or purpose, always with a grave, pasha-like 'we', now encouraging graciously, now admonishing sternly; and for others it was evidently ironic, merely joking, paying no attention and striving for the cheap glory of the *amuseur*; for some dried up old private lecturers this was even magisterial, every day invariably reiterating the dogma of some literary scholar or other. Only in two weeklies, the *Nation*[48] under the name M. Kent, the *Gegenwart*[49] under the cypher MH, were there discussions of the stage that had a modern touch and were not too distant from Jules Lemaître, Anatole France, Octave Mirbeau[50]. This M. Kent and this MH was an unknown youth without an Adah, who avoided the cliques, and those who enquired about him would hear that he had talent but that it was unfortunately merely recalcitrant and, refusing to adhere to convention, would not find its way. Such were the beginnings of Maximilian Harden.

Admittedly his manner did run contrary to convention, and those who measured it by the customary standards were horrified. He did not 'align' himself with the reliable norms of immutable aesthetics, quoted neither Aristotle nor Lessing, at most the worthy Frenzel[51], and then only to irreverently pluck his beard, did not follow a 'school', proclaimed no 'ism', and often the worthy populace, which in Berlin one might assume to be intelligent, would come to the end of four columns without knowing if it was praise or censure that they had just read. For the works of artists he did not even have, as Georg Brandes[52] once said of himself, the botanist's zeal for plants that he wishes to define and categorise. He helplessly succumbed to that *critique subjective et personnel* which so offends old Ferdinand Brunetière[53]. In fact he did not even discuss the artists and their works that he was 'criticising', rather he merely used these artists, these works to talk about himself, and only about himself; he wished to do with reviews what others do with poems, plays and stories. He treated the topic at hand the way the Goethe of the *Italian Journey*[54] treats that country and that people whom he does not so much portray as employ as a pretext, both stimulus and subject matter, for expressing himself, his own longing and his own joy and all that one's nerves and senses might experience. So in fact he was a good critic in the sense defined by Anatole France's formulation: '*Le bon critique est celui qui raconte les aventures de son* âme *au milieu des chefs-d'œuvre.*[55]' Except that it was not always *chefs-d'œuvre* that determined the adventures of his soul. But then – there was nothing he could do about that.

The Berliners were quite taken aback by this lyrical criticism and did not how to interpret it, but because it amused them they did not take it seriously; to respect they must be bored. This scarcely bothered him, and any warning from alarmed friends that he would not match the likes of Paul Lindau[56] merely stoked his defiance. The strangest theatre reviews one could imagine, often more akin to prose poems, often mocking satires, with teasing references to recent events, sketches from the street, caricatures from the salon, and touching upon a thousand things as his mood dictated and, by his own hand, without his ever having truly planned or reflected upon it, his writing became conversational, what the French call *chronique*. Without first waiting for a critical opportunity, he began commenting on the findings of the week, the reviewer became a *chroniqueur*, and then came the famous essays of 'Apostata'[57] which thrilled and outraged the Kaiserhof[58], and then the whole city, as no German journalist had ever thrilled or outraged before.

For a time he enjoyed it. He enjoyed learning all the means of this trade, all the technical tricks and schemes that formed the daily drill of Albert Wolff, Émile Blavet and Henry Fouquier[59], with whom he could soon confidently compare in his easy grace and brazen verve. He enjoyed ruffling the feathers of all manner of big names each week and sharpening that fatal word that would become the talk of the following eight days. But for all his appearance of jollity, in the long run the artificial jests of this *esprit fabriqué* did not satisfy his strict and truthful instincts, and in the long run as well, because this was Berlin, which has unaffiliated groups, which lacks society and mondaine living, there was insufficient material, and he recognised the danger that he might soon be writing for that one clique, café or table that alone could understand his otherwise cryptic allusions. He needed a theme that would touch the temperament of every German – his *chronique* became political.

He used politics like a painter uses paint, because that corner up there could still do with a bright spot, as the poet uses a thought, because its rich sound carries the rhythm, as the gymnast uses a pole, to demonstrate his lissom strength. It provided him with the best effects. He seeks current material and there was nothing more current than the ill-advised experiments of the young Kaiser who so vociferously desired fame.

The political *chroniqueur* is always polemical and always in opposition. He has to be. The technique demands it. Otherwise, one cannot function in this profession. Affirmation offers nothing to the wit, the swiftest mind is slowed in the defensive. Anyone promoting a cause is best advised to avoid the *chronique.*

There was no question that he would have to go into opposition. The only question was, which one? He could join the democrats or the socialists and for a time it seemed, indeed, as though he wished to become a second Mehring[60], only more agile and more fresh than that venerable old stick of radical negation. But he was too strong, too self-determined and too conscious of his self-determination to conform to the mould of a party, and he had a personal feel for people and for things that did not fit the ready phrases of political dogma. To be effective on his own, he had to go into opposition; but to avoid losing himself he could not join a party. He needed an opposition of his own, which belonged to none but himself, which brought him into opposition against the government and against all parties, and which was not a quirk, but rather a disposition. And in this disposition he found a new relationship to politics – he invented the opposition from above.

Before him we only had the opposition from below. Once one said to the government, 'You, government, you want it because it benefits you; but I, party of the peasants or of the bourgeoisie, must contest it because it harms me.' One set one's own advantage against that of the government. But now he explained instead, 'You, deceived government, wish for what harms you, and I use my higher reason to contest it because I wish to help you.' He set the true advantage of the government against its supposed advantage. He evaluated it by its own needs and desires. He judged as a king judges his uneducated princely sons who yet misjudge the duties of their station, deceived by false appearances. It was at this point that he would meet Bismarck, to whom a life spent in power admitted of no other criticism, and it was at this point that he came into such conflict with the Kaiser, who preferred malice and mockery from anyone rather than this educator.

Beneath the short, tight curls the bare, smooth face of the actor remains. He bears some resemblance to Kainz[61]; it is just that his sensitive features are even more mutable, more fleeting and more nervous. They change with every thought only to immediately slip away again, and should you wish to capture them in drawing, you would constantly feel that his frightened face were merely blinking in the sun. There is defiance and mockery about the mouth, from which a narrow chin falls soft and weary, and beneath his brow creased in perpetual rage he often looks like a wounded boy, not sure if he should weep or rampage, sullen and distressed, complaining that everyone keeps annoying him and he always has to defend himself, when he would rather be good and play. There is something womanly about him, in his uneven gestures, now shy, now fierce, in his fine, scuttling gait, in the gentle, mild, kind voice that can chirrup the most appalling things without guile. One has to be wary and one seldom knows how anything is intended, because his eye retains the same severe, objective look all along, and there is barely a revealing whisper about his soft lips, and often he himself is

ANTISEMITISM

unable to determine where the irony actually ends.

We are sitting outside the Café Bellevue[62], which looks out onto Leipziger Platz. I prefer to interview others – one is never sure with him; in the end he interviews back. Nor does he have the easy order of a trained mind, into which one need merely throw the question at the top, as in an automaton, to receive an immediate answer with the next jolt, rather he is a vagabond of chatter who often wanders off the carriageway to see whether there might not be something of interest in the adjacent woods.

I tell him the plan for the interview, and what Mommsen, from whom I have just come, had said – that he compared antisemitism to cholera.

He laughs, with a little mockery. 'Incidentally – let us stay with this image for now. It may serve us well. He is right – antisemitism is really a most filthy and ugly phenomenon, certainly not normal or healthy. But it is here, and the question is: how are we to rid ourselves of it? Is it reasonable, when cholera prevails, to stand in the market square, preaching against the disease as a disgrace to humanity and indignantly proclaiming shame and dishonour on all who have cholera? Do you think cholera would be at all bothered by that? Do you think that moral pathos can help or heal? Complaints and jeremiads achieve nothing, instead one must ask: what is to blame, where does the disease come from, how can one contain it and prevent relapse? One must listen to the teachings of the disease and supply good water, clean roads and condemn the filthy dwellings. So I say: you have to listen to the teachings of antisemitism and, in order to cast it out and preserve ourselves from it in the future, provide a clean economy and respectable morals.'

'So in fact you are – an antisemite to ward off antisemitism?'

'I am not at all an antisemite, I am …'

'But everyone believes you to be.'

'Because I am against the middle-man spirit, against the stock market mob, against the putrid egotism of the bourgeoisie! Can I help it if people call that anti-semitic? Can I help it if Jewry declares its solidarity with the Wolffs, Leipzigers and Sommerfelds[63]? Can I help it if one cannot speak out against the mercantile spirit without immediately being considered in league with the Ahlwardts? One strikes out at capital and – the Jew feels affected! It is no wonder, then, that ultimately popular opinion can no longer distinguish between capital and Jew and it is quite forgotten that it is among the greatest sons of Shem, among Acosta and Spinoza, Börne and Heine, Lassalle and Marx[64], that 'aversion to traders and Jews as such' as Börne once said[65], aroused the most vio-lent passion. Today it is the Jews themselves who cause antisemitism by being fool enough to use capitalist fraud as a shield to deflect all blows. When they themselves say, 'anyone who is opposed to exploitation and middlemen is opposed to Jews', one cannot hold it against people who conclude, 'well, if capital and Jew are the same, then yes, we are against the Jews as well'. And the thousands of good, righteous and often scrupulously untainted Jews who themselves, as the good, clean Lasker once did, indignantly damn the banditry of the bedraggled sons of Plutus, and although innocent must pay the price! But why do they not rise up and protest this conflation of stock market fraud and Judaism? What do the stock market and usury have to do with religion and race? The clerical Bontoux[66] was not much better than our Friedländer and Sommerfeld[67], and I gladly return to the clever phrase that the morally sound heroine utters in *L'Argent*: "*Pour moi, les juifs, ce sont des hommes comme les autres. S'ils sont à part, c'est qu'on les y a mis.*"[68] I repeat it against the antisemites and against the Jews – against the antisemites, who wish to set all Jewry ablaze when a Jew steals; against the Jews, who believe theft should be sanctified because a Jew has stolen. Whether Jews or Christians, we aim to combat the corrupting omnipotence of capitalism and the dogma of Manchester and strive for healthier, purer, righteous conditions – then we shall have marital harmony between Jews and Germans, which is a little harder for us than for others because there are homoeopathic similarities to be found here; the Jew and the German are too similar.'

MORITZ VON EGIDY

All the signs point to humanity turning religious once more. Perhaps it is only a brief fashion, like the Romantics and their brief strike against the Enlightenment; perhaps it will endure. The Salvation Army and other sects are forming; Tolstoy's[69] call to faith is finding disciples; the Theosophical[70] movement is growing; the spiritualists are multiplying their communities; in France a new Catholicism is on the rise and the Germans are renewing their Protestantism. Young people are no longer satisfied with the cheap words of the scientific rationalists; they mock Büchner and Vogt[71]. 'Against Materialism' is the name of a society in Munich, and in Berlin there is an 'Ethical Society'[72]. People crave emotion, they seek ethos. They are turning away from cold reason. They want a grand obligation once again. They are shifting from the individual to the whole and wish to forget themselves and serve others – or perhaps they serve others precisely so that they may lose themselves. It probably is just a fashion; but it could also be the great change in spirit, the leave-taking of this century that heralds the next.

But in this growing religious inclination there are two impulses that are quite distinct, which are in fact contradictory. There are those who, lost in Catholic rhapsody, covet faith like chloral, as a congenial anaesthetic that gives one strange dreams, withdrawing from the stale reality of miserable life and drawing fantastical, profound, strange stimuli from forgotten fiery liturgies. Others seek moral aid, they are the followers of the Russian novels and, in Germany, Lieutenant Colonel von Egidy, and they wish for an end to the crazed play on their nerves and the coming of calm power in active transfiguration and for a more exhilarating life based on dependable guiding standards. They wish to forget, become intoxicated, suffocate in faith. Through it they wish to awaken to the practice of recognised responsibilities and draw meaning from a life sanctified by good works.

Mr von Egidy is regarded as an educator and teacher of the people, and many are those who hasten to hear his words and seek his counsel, and profess his laws. He first dealt with questions of religion alone in his *Earnest Thoughts*[73], which appeared in autumn 1890, by explaining the separation of Christian values from the Church's doctrines, or 'Churchism', and in so doing called for a vital 'Jesusism' of the deed for every individual, one that relies not on conviction and confession, but on faithful transformation through pious, moral, God-fearing works; by denying the rule of dogma, he wished to reconcile the denominations and achieve a 'united Christianity'. But by faithfully following the urging of his teachings the churchman soon became a social reformer. Taking Christianity 'seriously' was his slogan, and he proclaimed, 'The power of a faith is measured solely by how forcefully it urges us to the conviction that the potential grounded in eternal law should become reality. The blessing of a faith is not that it leads us out of reality into a sphere of ideas – the blessing of a faith is proven solely in the urge that guides us to goodness. If I pray, "Lord, strengthen my faith," I am not expressing the wish that my reason be veiled so that I may absorb anew ideas I once thought self-evident because they were taught to me; with this prayer I am instead striving for inner clarity, to visualise my God-given conditions, and I am struggling for the confidence that such states will come to be ... And it is only this faith that leads to action, and only in action does faith become a thing of value for humanity.' And so he had to call for an 'applied' Christianity: 'Laws, ordinances, institutions and measures must emanate from a Christ-like disposition, and may therefore themselves be nothing but pure, devoted, selfless love; that is because those who live by such laws can only be good, and will choose to be good.' Because he only recognised true religion in actions, he had to become an apostle of reform: 'We must create conditions that make trespass impossible, conditions that do not even provoke or arouse the desire for injustice; and before long we shall have no more need of punishment.'

The movement that comes from his writings is constantly growing. A large part of the nobility and the officer class follow it; German Freemasonry, led by Professor Settegast, the founder of the Grand Lodge of Prussia, known as 'Kaiser Friedrich for Covenant Loyalty'[74], recognises a kindred spirit; the socialists maintain friendly relations with it. And in the journal *United Christianity*, led by Kiel Professor Lehmann-Hohenberg[75] in service of the movement, you can read a list of the many essays, books and speeches written about it.

Moabit[76]. It is the quarter for assessors who drill rich rogues for exams, of officials with long titles and short salaries, of modest pensions. This is where the legal little people live, and the good, neat bourgeoisie peer from their bright houses. There is a shimmer and glitter to the stairs and the walls, bright flashes, and a thin, light vapour steaming as though after the rain. It is the kind of scrubbed, rinsed atmosphere you often find in the paintings of Kuehl, Walter Firle, Dora Hitz[77].

He is short and stout. He is not what I expected of an imperturbable optimist with passion, impetus and enthusiasm. You might take him for a retired military man who has spent his entire life thinking of nothing but drilling his recruits, for one of those short, fat, asthmatic majors who are quick to anger, crimson and cursing. His bearing is straight and stiff, with sparse, terse, imperious gestures. He speaks as one issuing a reprimand or command to an assembled corps. Short, sharp, irrefutable, every word like a command in itself, with hard, abrupt pauses. He does not adapt his turns of phrase to those of his partner, who may stray from the matter at hand and may first wish to chat a little, the better to draw out his nature; he does not deviate from his topic and seems always to pursue a prepared concept without interruption. When you say something, he tilts his wrinkled forehead a little, peers critically into space and soon interrupts with a firm, clear gesture, decisive and final. All the while he is uncommonly polite. But those who are accustomed to the soft, conversational, yielding disposition of 'fine society' find him brittle and hard.

In his presence one has a strange blend of feelings which refuse to coalesce. It also takes time to find the right measure, the right value for him. You cannot measure him against the expectations that arise from his writings. In place of the fiery enthusiast of your assumption there is a stiff, fervent gentleman who pursues ethics with the pedantic vehemence of the angler, stamp-collector or butterfly enthusiast, and major ideas are presented almost like minor quirks. Even spirit and wit and that graceful talent of always presenting oneself to the guest in all the high arts are better mastered by trifling idlers. Yet he commands respect. You feel superior, and yet there is awe, envy almost. Often a wonderful tone will arise all of a sudden; when he speaks of the 'good cause', of the 'noble people', his voice assumes a warmth and transfiguration, a radiance and a brightness, as from a bright joy in the breast, the possession of which must be delectable. He may lack the vanities of *esprit* but one feels that he has power and greatness of conscience.

There is a small room filled with his pamphlets and speeches, with the journals of the associations that serve him, with the writings of friends who cherish the same hopes and desires, of Colonel von Gizycki, Heinrich Hart, Wilhelm von Polenz[78] who aspire with him to that state of 'united Christianity', 'in which righteousness and truthfulness, humanity, and mutual respect prevail'.

Then he introduces me to his family in a bright, wide room. A quiet, slender, pale woman sits and embroiders, issuing fine and surreptitious words, goodly and mild, like diffident dragonflies. A small table is covered in white, and three blond girls, lightly dressed, glide softly like scuttling sun rays. There is peace unutterable.

He will gladly offer his opinion on antisemitism. But he does not approve of interviews. 'When I speak to my fellow human beings, I wish to think over every word precisely and thoroughly, to measure its meaning completely, to consider its effect at length and examine whether it could be interpreted differently, whether it says too much or too little, whether I could find a better one that avoids all doubt. Through rigorous care I wish to attain the surety that I can answer to every single word at any time. But this I can only achieve with pen in hand, striking through, hesitating over and over again. In speaking one may easily let slip a word that carelessly disfigures the meaning.'

So for the opinions he has offered he presents a formula that he considers to be just and effective:

'As long as antisemitism holds fast to its name, and to an outlook that is so pitiable to us Germans, that holds that half a million of another race are ravishing fifty million of our own, the healthy, vigorous and just man will see nothing more in the entire movement than the expression of an un-Christian attitude, which seeks to impose its own guilt about our deplorable conditions on a defenceless minority.

It is only in that moment when the impure tone of antisemitism dissolves in the serious *antimalum* accord, that is, in the moment when we combat the evil, the wrong, the untrue, the unjust, the unfair, the unholy – in a word, the un-Christlike – wherever and in whomever we find it, regardless of race or faith, but with no coldness to the evildoer himself, who is only ever a result of our conditions – from that moment on, all righteous people will join in the mighty battle cry: against evil!

The destruction of evil means the victory of goodness. Our conditions shall be ruled by Christian reason; reasonable religiosity shall teach people to unite in a single need for sanctification. Sectarianism is a thing of the past. From that point there will be nothing to prevent those people who still call themselves Jews today from combining religiously – and now also racially – with the host peoples whose lands they have inhabited for centuries. Judaism is merging into the civilised nations, thus fulfilling its purpose for the development of the human race.

Berlin, 31 March 1893.
M. v. Egidy.'

ERNST HAECKEL

I am staying in the 'Bär', where Luther once stayed, and where last year Bismarck intoned his legacy unto the Germans: 'It is a dangerous experiment today to strive for absolutist desires in the heart of Europe ... What we must strive for in the future is an increase in political trust, in public opinion and in parliament[79].' Where jubilation once rang out it is now very lonely, quiet and cosy. Tiny blossoms sway outside as I recover from the journey in comfort with a bright, cool, mild Pisporter wine, and a brown bust shines against the grey wall, and I rack my brains trying to work out whether the bronze is one of the great students or a teacher, or which poet it may be. But it is Mr Friedrich Gottlob Schulze, the 'founder of the agriculture union schools in Jena.' One never ceases to learn.

I order a coach. But 'today there are no more cabs; the students have gone out to the country.' So I slowly stroll through the town to his house on the out-skirts, on Bergstrasse.

At some point I should like to stroll there with Maurice Barrès, the clever virtuoso of 'enthusiasms', chatting and gazing upon these narrow, barren, sober streets, where there is little more than a few nooks, scrolls and spires stirring on the dry and sleepy houses, and even the meagre Gothic of the wan church fails to make an impression. As hardship struck the fatherland it was here that the holy zeal of the *Burschenschaft*[80] was born. What manner of men who, with no stimulus or assistance from others, summoned the most powerful sentiments from within themselves! What heroes! What artists! They had none of our contrivances of disposition.

I could not say if today's students here resemble them. The few who had not left for the country do not strike me as such. They are smug and fantastically fastidious, with the solemn politesse of the fearless famulus Wagner, who in our time would be a government clerk, and from his scrupulous, shining centre parting and his gleaming tie it is clear that today's student is 'an enemy of all roughness'[81].

Perhaps the true grandsons of the fraternity are only to be found among the professors. In his drive, courage and loyalty to freedom, Ernst Haeckel is one of them. Just think how angry and reckless he was last year, when Minister Zedlitz-Trützschler tried to 'divest the elementary school of scientific pedagogy and deliver it to the papist hierarchy with hands tied', when he came out against the '*Weltanschauung* of the new course'[82], when he countered arguments with a charge of lèse-majesté.

Young birches shimmer around the quiet house, a Schinkel-esque structure rising sober and noble on a hill. The gardener is working in the flower beds. All is solemn, fine, serene.

He is lying on a long black sofa before a large table laden with books and papers, catalogues, his *History of Creation*[83] and my interviews in the *Deutsche Zeitung*. He sprained his foot on the journey home from Italy, and it hurts when he moves. The room is broad and wide and open, you feel yourself to be in a bright forest where the smooth trunks do not crowd in; white flowers stir at the window.

There is nothing at all of the professor about him, nothing at all of the 'grim faces of the scholars' that Schiller once found in Jena[84]. He is all strength, freedom and joy. You might take him for a rambler, a gymnast, a hunter, for a person of the *plein air* persuasion who delights in activity; he is transfigured by pleasure, health and kindness. It is that last joy which Nietzsche wished to dream, and I think of the Rembrandt German[85] when he speaks of his 'strong and gentle hero', and – strange in such a German setting – there is a French song I cannot get out of my mind, having recently picked it up somewhere:

> *'Jeune, j'étais trop sage,*
> *Et voulais tout savoir;*
> *Je veux à mon âge*
> *Que badinage.'* [86]

He offers his opinions and arguments with passionate zeal, as a collector displays his treasures, constantly moving on because he cannot wait, returning a second and third time, so that one can examine it more thoroughly and really see it from every side.

'Of course there is nothing I can tell you. Who could, on this question that has already been discussed a thousand times over? But at least I have complete impartiality on my side. On the one hand, I have had many Jewish friends for years, whom I adore and cherish – they are wonderful, magnificent people – which is why the usual abuse of the Jews cannot reach me, because I have learned better. On the other hand, some of my best and brightest pupils are vehement antisemites, so I say to myself, again from my own experience, that one cannot excuse it as ignorance and crudity, and I do not agree with Mommsen's declaration that antisemitism is an aberration and a disease. I cannot believe, my entire outlook resists the idea that such a powerful, enduring and extensive movement should be entirely without grounds. Instead I lean more towards Schmoller's view, which rightly assumes it to be a national issue – that very much appealed to me. The religious and social elements seem to me of little importance. It is a racial issue. It cannot be denied that in some things we regard the Jews as alien and that they feel themselves to be alien – that should not be taken as a reproach against them; it cannot be otherwise considering their history, the way conditions have developed throughout history. At a time when the national element is so powerful, this of course leads to conflict, and I believe that the power of this national element will actually increase in the near future, lamented though it may be by a higher, cosmopolitan idealism. I have just seen it again in Italy. When I think back to 1859, before Garibaldi – well, a Sicilian would never have considered himself Italian. Only in the north did people begin to feel a sense of nationhood. And so it is in every country. Cosmopolitanism is still out of reach. For the time being, national sentiment is still increasing, strengthening everywhere …'

'Except in France … especially not in Paris. There the youth do not wish to know about the national element at all, and those who are truly modern think in a highly cosmopolitan way.'

'But ultimately that is only one city. Otherwise everything today is distinguished by the national element more than ever. And from this perspective antisemitism becomes quite understandable – not, of course, the antisemitic agitation that we all must lament and condemn – no decent, educated person could be an adherent of Ahlwardtism – but it is understandable that one no longer tolerates the foreign nature of the Jews in the midst of the people, that one may wish to remove the specifically Jewish part of them and educate them in German habits and customs until they are like unto the people with whom they live in every respect. That is the legitimate aspect of antisemitism, that the Jews should abandon their peculiarities and completely merge with us – anyone who feels and thinks in a national sense must demand that of them.'

'But do you not think that the antisemitic movement is delaying rather than fostering precisely that close fusion, which every intelligent person must desire?'

'Every movement has its merits and its perils. I consider it a merit of antisemitism that it has awoken in the Germans and in the Jews the conviction that Jews must relinquish their special nature and become entirely German in their morals, customs and sentiments. We must tirelessly pursue this goal and prevent the entry of new and often morally questionable elements from the East who disrupt the process of making them German. It is in the interests of our many distinguished, upright, and honourable Jews in particular that I should like to see Jewish immigration from the East impeded, and I wonder whether that wretched lot are not most undesirable to the decent and civilised Jews themselves, those who honestly consider themselves Germans, for arousing mistrust and delaying their complete absorption into our race. False humanity does nought but harm here, and I think we should vigorously protect ourselves against the Russian Jews, not because they are Jews, but because they are incompatible with our civilisation – just as the Californians protect themselves against the Chinese[87]; the ideal of love for 'everything that bears a human countenance' unfortunately fails in practice. Last year I took the boat to England and I saw Russian emigrants of that sort; their filth and vulgarity were inexpressible, and the English were quite right to simply not admit them into their country. It is precisely in the interest of educated Jews, against whom such unclean elements only incite hatred and exasperation – I emphasise this expressly, because I consider these purified and noble Jews to be important factors in German culture; for it should not be forgotten that they always stood bravely for the Enlightenment and freedom in the face of reaction; reliable combatants who often stood against the obscurantists, and amid the perils of this terrible time, when there is such a powerful revival of papistry afoot, we cannot do without their proven courage.'

ADOLPH WAGNER

Once upon a time I attended his seminars, for two years.[88] This is how I know him. And I have great respect and admiration for him.

From student to teacher this is hardly surprising. More surprising is everything else that befalls him. Those who know him only from the lectern, from the podium, do not like him, even those of his disposition and his faction. Those who get close to him wax lyrical, even those who do not share his views. He alienates from afar. He seduces from close quarters. He is one of those people you have to see at home to understand. Out there, before a crowd, he appears as an unfortunate enigma. In his chamber, among his books, when he argues with his abrupt, sharp, pointed gestures in the rapid, narrow twang of his words, he has no difficulty explaining himself, and one loves him because one recognises his blind, naive, devoted submission to every mood. This is an individual formed of nothing but temperament. He is defined by momentary sentiments. He cannot stand the reins of reason, consideration or hesitation, and abides by the most recent sensation until he is suddenly seized by another – newer, stronger – and driven elsewhere. The stranger, who only ever sees the outcome, is powerless to interpret it and turns peevish. The friend who is witness to this boiling, simmering, steaming temperament is forced to admire the moral impressionist.

For he is indeed a moral impressionist, one who obeys every momentary urge, always putting his strength and his drive, his entire nature at the service of his most recent sensations. But this is always determined by his irritable, intolerant, imperious and upright nature, which is far from clubbable. Moving along the row he will see only that one delicate point that offends the defenceless, and he will pit himself against it. He is always opposed to the crowd, the 'compact majority'[89], prevailing opinion; he is always in favour of those who are misjudged and unjustly suppressed. When it was still a matter of course in his guild to swear by traditional economics and mock the demands of the workers, he turned to radical social-ism, and then, when the fashion for socialism spread among the professors, he became a critical, thoughtful voice of warning. He is a born defender of the weak and born champion against the powerful.

This may derive from a lust for conflict rather than a sense of justice. It guides him, it seduces him. He has a belligerent strain that cannot resist the temptation of the feud. The issue itself is minor, and for him it is not about the victory. He loves the metier of combat. He only comes alive when he argues. He only feels when he can measure himself against his enemies. He needs the tumult and turmoil of contradictions. He is a truly a mercenary in spirit.

It was often highly amusing in his seminars. He did not care for the obedient disciples who blindly worshipped the master's teachings. He would listen impatiently, fidget in his armchair, click his tongue, and one saw how he was driven to seek out contradictions. But he enjoyed the queer ones who were entrenched in their quirks and gave absolutely no thought to conversion. And if some mischief-maker impishly praised the lesson he had just given and exaggerated a little out of enthusiasm, we sometimes found the master irritably departing from his own dogma and deploying the most hostile evidence against his own theses.

He resembles Clemenceau a little in his rash movements and nimble expressions. Every gesture, every word has an edge, and he casts his phrases like arrows. He launches into conversation as though he were in the boxing ring and lurking as you speak, looking out for the weak spot. He wishes to provoke you. Much is merely feint, so that you may twist and lose your footing.

I try to tell him what has brought me to him today, but he immediately scolds me. 'Oh!? Naturally! You need me – and so here you are again. Otherwise you have not cared a fig for me all this time! How long has it been?'

'Seven, eight years …'

'And in the meantime you were back in Berlin – because you wrote those horrid pieces, at the *Freie Bühne*[90], or whatever it is called. Are you still writing those horrid pieces?'

'Yes. Incessantly. Another one recently in Vienna. That was even more horrid.'

'How nice for you! And do you really think you can outdo Goethe and Schiller with them?'

'No, not yet. But actually it was not about Naturalism that I wished to interview you, but antisemitism.'

'What? You want what?'

'Just a little gentle interviewing ... about ...'

'Quite the most appalling fashion we are now copying from the Americans ...'

'It is not the Americans I am copying, but the French.'

'That is even worse! Yes – that is what they told me, that you are mad for the French now!'

'I prefer them to the Prussians.'

'And why? A people of prattlers, fools and buffoons who live on nothing but words and are incapable of honest labour ...! How can you now, after the most recent trials, with the ghastly degeneration ...'

'Ah, because of a little corruption? You have it here as well! The German Panama seems ...'[91]

'German Panama! It is such an exaggeration to speak of a German Panama – and there is no trace, not the slightest cause for such a comparison. Well, now I really know your ways!'

'The expression is not mine. The expression is from Hertwig[92] and Ahlwardt – from your party ...'

'Firstly, I do not belong to any party now; I do not care for politics any more – I have had my fill of it. I wish to live for my scholarship alone now. I resist any temptation to be dragged back into political dispute. I spoke publicly again the other day – in favour of the Army Bill; but that is not political but patriotic. And I refute absolutely any commonality with Ahlwardt. I do not know this individual, but from what I hear of him, he is simply a – but I ought to be on my guard! You will put it in the newspaper and then it is I who will have the bother and annoyance.'

'Do you believe that his documents …?'

'Documents! How can you call them documents! Old tittle-tattle – a brochure from Rudolf Meyer, who always screamed and raged and then, when it came to court, proved nothing! Ahlwardt is – but one cannot say anything in the presence of one who immediately writes it all down for the newspaper! Which newspaper are you doing it for?'

'For the *Deutsche Zeitung*.'

'But that is liberal! They will only rail against me! And then that spreads throughout the entire press, and everyone adds his portion of wisdom, and I get heartily sick of it. I am entirely disgusted by politics. I wish for peace. And why are you coming to me anyway? Go to the political leaders!'

'You are one.'

'Not any more.'

'You are still considered one of the leaders of antisemitism.'

'I am not that at all. I never was. I am Christian-Social. But I have never advocated antisemitism as it is understood today. I hold that an antisemitism that conflates the social question with the Jewish question is wrong. A solution to the Jewish question would by no means solve the social question, which would remain exactly the same were we to have no Jews at all. But people rail against the Jew and they mean the capitalist. That makes no sense. That one should combat the excesses of capitalism, dishonest acquisition, stock market fraud through taxes and reforms – by all means! But what does that have to do with the Jews? Perhaps that the deficiencies of capitalism sometimes appear even more embarrassing in Jewish form, that I would not contest. But that does not strike at the heart of the question. The social question remains the same, with or without Jews, and demands its own solution, which may also apply to this or that Jew, just as it applies to capitalist Christians, but has nothing to do with Judaism in itself. That is what I have always preached.'

'Then why do people call you an antisemite?'

'Because the Jews always identify with capitalism! If you speak out against capital, they act as if one had insulted their religion. And in a sense I am antisemitic anyway. I cannot stand the Jewish nature, Jewish bad habits, and I believe in any case that they may bring danger to German customs. Look at the Jewish women on the street, how they dress and behave! That surely arouses a certain aesthetic antisemitism – we perceive them as an alien race which offends our taste and our habits. In this sense every German is an antisemite, no honest person can deny it. But then of course – I do not know what to do about it either. It is just the same with socialism; in their critique the socialists are usually right, but when one turns to them for positive assistance, they do not know what to do either. Then they shroud themselves in mystical silence and trust everything to development, that all will resolve itself. But that counts for nothing at all. Without the active zeal of individuals there is no development, and a critique that does not at the same time provide practical assistance is of no value. It is just the same with the Jews. I admit it: the Jews are repugnant and offend our tastes. But what then? What becomes of us? What should we do? We cannot kill them, or drive them from our land. Somehow we just have to swallow it. At most one might consider making immigration from the East harder, or the like. But one must never believe, as the antisemites do, that this would solve the social question, or would even come close to solving it in any way. The social issue is a problem in its own right that has nothing to do with the Jews.'

PRINCE HEINRICH
ZU SCHOENAICH-CAROLATH

The prince was 18 years old when the Germans marched on France; after the Liegnitz Ritterakademie he joined the army and served throughout the entire war with the Fifteenth Hussars. But his gift for gentle brooding drew him to science. He began studying in Bonn. Since 1877 he has been Councillor for the district of Guben[93], since 1881 a member of the Reichstag. He first belonged to the Free Conservatives[94], but left the party because his sensitive conscience could not endure constraint. These days, especially, many pin their hopes on him, and his attempt to reconcile the Huene proposal with the desire for shortened service[95] appears to have saved the Army Bill and the duration of the service at the last minute.

He is Lord of the dynastic free state Amtitz and the dominion of Starzeddel in Lower Lusatia, hereditary member of the Prussian ruling house and Captain *à la suite* of the army.

I meet him in the Parliament, and it is not easy

to find an undisturbed corner right away. In the long, narrow room where the grey walls are adorned with bas-reliefs of famous patriots amid their strongest and greatest axioms, chattering, counselling, arguing groups are crowding around while in the hall they are crying slanderer, scoundrel and coward. Next door they are dishing up generous portions at white table settings. We are forced to venture upstairs. There a fat gentleman is lying on a black sofa smoking a great post of a cigar; peering in from the door and seeing only the firm sphere of the enormous abdomen, with the smoke rising darkly behind it, it presents a fantastically cynical picture, with a hint of the rough caricatures of Forain[96]. Next door they are reading and writing. So we wander amid the lounging servants, and only on the top floor do we find an empty, wide, quiet room; there is a faint buzz from Leipziger Strasse[97].

When you see him before you, his short, swift, sharp gait and his terse, supple posture make him seem quite youthful, and he has the brown, free, happy face of a rider; only the melancholy mildness of his shy, slow gaze and his grey hair age him a little. He is very polite, almost womanly in his solicitude for his guest, with a faint shimmer of that goodly awkwardness of the great, who are intent on avoiding the appearance of conceit at all costs, and become self-conscious out of sheer eagerness to remove the self-consciousness of the other. It takes some time for the hesitant words to flow; he pauses frequently, ponders and ruminates at length. He is calm and gentle in his speech, but from it shines forth a noble cheer, that quiet joy of Johannes Rosmer[98] that 'ennobles the senses'. He combines strict Prussian rigour, the worldly, light grace of good society, and the quiet elegance of action provided by the peace of a clear conscience. That enchantment exuded by good men combines exquisitely with the most distinguished forms of noble upbringing.

His zeal swells as he talks. It is a fine thing, watching him warm up and grow indignant against evildoing. The words rise, bold and unyielding.

'I deeply regret that the issue of antisemitism has arisen anew and is once again posing questions that, after all, have long been settled for any educated person. Sons of the same fatherland should not be feuding, and in their rights as well as their duties there should and must be no difference. We demand the same love for the monarchy from the Jews, the same devotion to the good of the state, the same bravery and sacrifice in times of distress and tribulation – thus we cannot withhold the same rights from them. Consequently, I will always oppose any attempt to legally restrict Jews and will combat the anti-semitic movement as a great danger to our entire culture, as it threatens to cast us back into the age of intolerance, which seemed to have been overcome by the efforts of the noblest and the best, by Lessing and Goethe, by Emperor Joseph II and Frederick the Great. It is incompatible with the notion of the modern state, which is founded on tolerance and acceptance, equal rights and equal duties for all, and I heartily lament that this movement is once again fuelling the political intolerance from which we now suffer. Our lack of objectivity is astonishing. No justice may be done to the adversary, and nobody wishes to indulge a different view, nobody wishes to acknowledge it as justified. In this, too, we should take England as a model; there politicians of the most varied parties associate amicably with one another and it is there that Gladstone, for instance, enjoys unreserved recognition from all parties for his talents and merits, and the keenest sympathy for his personal well-being, even though the majority find his Irish plans wholly disagreeable and irksome. This is what we should aspire to and become accustomed to, even with those opponents separated from us by the opposition of party and faction, while always following our own convictions and respecting the goodwill of all who serve their fatherland in their own way. I sincerely strive to treat all views fairly. But I can also tell you a thing or two about the political hostility of our opponents, which according to German custom usually also extends to one's private life, more's the pity. But this cannot and must not deter anyone who, according to honest conviction, without secondary intentions or aspirations, pursues his own path and has no intention other than to fulfil his duty to the best of his beliefs. So I regret and bemoan the antisemitic movement, and I confidently hope that the waves now lapping will recede over time and yield to a fairer, more proper, more humane understanding. During my frequent trips abroad and in my dealings with foreign statesmen, politicians and private individuals, I have often seriously wondered how this movement could have assumed such significance among us, and how it could encompass so many groups. And then it seems to me that in England, and probably in other countries as well, those peculiarities of the Jewish race that are less agreeable and congenial are erased faster than they are here. We see in other countries, too, followers of the Mosaic faith fully absorbed into society and into the political system, which has admittedly granted them full equality. There they regard themselves as elements of the whole, parts of the whole and indivisibly bound to the whole. Unfortunately, I feel that this is not always the case in Germany, perhaps because not enough time has elapsed since the Jews were granted equality. Maybe that is the sole reason that they have not yet assimilated as they have elsewhere, and now antisemitism is giving rise to a new disturbance, an aggravation of contrasts and the danger of further alienation. In the interests of the state, we must demand that the Jews act for the public good in the same way and with exactly the same warmth as the Christians do, and that on no account should they regard themselves as foreign in any way. But the necessary, ineluctable precondition for this is their complete equality. I hope that when it is fully achieved and accomplished, that some of the peculiarities of the Jews that have offered just cause for criticism will disappear. The more the Jewish tribe assimilates with the German, the sooner it will lose those peculiarities that at times offend our feelings. In my opinion, full equality is, as I said, the only effective means, whereas any exception in the state and in society widens the gap. This is what antisemitism does, and therefore in the interests of the state and from a humanist point of view I hold it to be reprehensible. And one more thing: to me it is the most peculiar manifestation of antisemitism that there should be so many alliances between prosperous Jewish women and persons from reputable families, who have so many antisemites among their ranks or among their relatives, who are often antisemites themselves! That seems very strange to me. And I think one should accept the consequences of one's actions here – each in his own way. There is so much more one could say about this …!'

HEINRICH RICKERT

The former deputy from Danzig has just turned sixty. He began as an unpaid city councillor, then in Königsberg he was elected Country Director of the Province of Prussia, but renounced this when the province was later divided[99]. He has been in the Prussian House of Representatives[100] since 1870, in the Reichstag since 1874 and otherwise lives between Danzig and Karlikau-Sopot.

He is an agile, swift politician, always there, always ready, never tiring. There are few who speak more often. His are not those great, considered, philosophical speeches with which the likes of Bennigsen[101] reckon with all the emotions of the populace before a decision to hold a last judgment of all the desires in the land; but he is a nimble speaker on the day, for the day, a quick-witted journalist of the podium. He does not shrink from the harshest words when they are required, but he deplores the enmity of the parties and would like to convey that each should respect the conviction of the other. He is friendly with many opponents, and the ample, cosy apartment out there in bright Tiergarten[102] often sees conservatives and democrats mingling agreeably over venerable old wines.

His group, the 'Rickert wing', is reputed to oppose the rule of Richter, which is said not to be wholly agreeable in its forms. They give him a free hand, only they think it is not always enough to know every item of the budget. They are more nationalist and then again closer to the socialists, who value them as reliable guardians of liberty and do not wish to combat them with such anger.

He has a long, powerful skull and his red face glows. His broad, frayed beard hangs from his drooping cheeks and his small, shrewd, bright eyes sparkle with such cunning and cheer that one might be tempted to call him a happy Silenus[103] if parliamentary respect did not forbid it. One may think of a genuine Forty-Eighter[104] with all democratic modesty and dignity, and at the same time those leisurely fellows painted by Böcklin, given to splashing around with mermaids[105].

I submit my request to him.

'My position on the Jewish question is well known. After all, I am the leader of the "Jew Protection Troop"[106] – with a 12,000-mark salary as Mr Ahlwardt announced today! Ah, what slander, what meanness, what filth! It is no wonder that one finally loses one's patience and one also says things that – well, I prefer not to think on it any longer ... Words cannot help against antisemitism. We need work. And you have to admit – we work hard, harder than they do. Just look at our statements! Often I think that maybe we can promote each other in some way. But unfortunately we do not have any connection with you, with your people. Austrian liberalism – for us it is something so strange, so distant, that we have no sense of it at all – we do not hear or see or know anything about it ...'

'Console yourself – nor do we ...'

'I have long had it in mind, and I always wanted to discuss it and enquire. You see, I am turning the tables – I am interviewing you.'

'About liberalism?'

'About liberalism in Austria.'

'I am afraid you will have no luck ...'

'Why, you do not care to?'

'I do care to, but I do not know if I can. It is a thing with our liberals – as the old song goes: they are here, they are there, but you cannot find them anywhere. They only appear for the elections – then one has the pleasure. Otherwise they disappear for the whole year and I really would not know ... You simply have to go to Lussinpiccolo[107] one time – there, if you are lucky, you might manage to catch one ... Why would you want a relationship with a party that has no relationship to itself?'

'But you must admit, it is strange that we have, for example, much better connections with the English Liberals than with you, with whom we have a common past and so many common interests. And how much might we help and benefit each other if we shared our experience and our plans? Just look at our opponents! The movement against liberalism is international. Soon our antisemites will come to you, soon one of your antisemites will speak here – it is a tireless back and forth;

things that work here are suggested there, and dangers identified there are avoided here. Why should we remain apart and separate while our opponents unite? But all attempts at rapprochement between our liberals and yours have been in vain.'

'Your idea strikes me as splendid – because our people really need a push from the outside to get moving again. It is our custom to do everything among two or three people at a time, and liberal politics has become a cumbersome mystery, where one must serve many, many years before one is ushered into the innermost sanctum of the "initiates". If one of you were to come to us now and then and converse with us poor devils as humans, that would lend us a little bravery in the face of the liberal pontiffs. But I do not know exactly what form you are considering.'

'Initially I am not considering any form that would be mere compulsion with no benefit. I simply feel that a certain number of us could come to you so many times a year, and so many of you to us – they must build the bridge of personal and functional communication. Everything else will arise from that. The sole concern is to engender a means by which we learn a little more from you and you from us, an exchange of opinions, experience and plans, to conclude and studiously maintain an unspoken yet reliable covenant which, I think, would serve as gratifying support to each.'

'What if you were to come to Vienna and speak publicly? …'

'No, not me … I am not thinking about myself in the whole thing at all …'

'So another of your party ... that would be the same after all. But he would have to speak publicly ... any subject – the 'tasks of liberalism' for example. That would be a sensation in Vienna. First, a large gathering of liberals there is a miracle in and of itself. Second, foreigners would once again raise liberalism above the level of Prague and Eger to which one presently wishes to reduce its international value entirely.'

'That could be done. Simply set the cause in motion! The most important thing remains that the parliamentary brethren here and there approach, and communicate with, each other – I believe this would result in the best of outcomes ... not least in the fight against an antisemitic society.'

JOHN HENRY MACKAY

It was back then, when I was writing all those wild things, raging against all coercion and domination, wishing for the same freedom for all men. That's when we became close, because the same passion, a wild yearning for a happier and nobler life roared in us both, and we exchanged letters, each rebuking the other and praising himself and solemnly swearing to use our powers in the service of humanity. We were in a hurry to break all order and create a better world.

He was living in Zurich. I was in Paris. I need not tell how I conducted myself there. It is recorded in a dear old book; everyone knows the 'Gypsy life' of Murger and Musette; Phenice and Mimi are unforgettable. There one may read the tone, the customs, the adventures of the 'Momus' café[108], where even the waiters were dumbstruck by the conversations of these philosophers, these artists in the prime of their lives. This gives a clear, accurate picture of how I lived, and in between I wrote those very wild things, especially when there was no more money in the house.

The great exhibition had just opened on the Champs de Mars[109], we were settled quite happily in our hotel, painters, poets, all important personages, each more decadent than the next, and the corresponding feminine contingent – suddenly I am presented with a card. A stranger wishes to speak to me. I read: John Henry Mackay – and I am terrified of the gloomy apostle of liberty, who might well ruin my hardly pessimistic situation. But he already knows that I am here, and there is nothing I can do.

He arrives. He looks more human than the fanatic I imagined. Certainly there are heavy, dull clouds on his mighty forehead. But when he sees the many bottles and the female contingent, he is visibly cheered and assuaged. We resume our revelry immediately and he readily takes part. Within ten minutes we are the best of friends. Within an hour we drink to brotherhood. And this night and the next we do not part and must surely have discussed important things.

We have remained good friends, although our careers kept us apart. He diligently maintained his wild urge for freedom and turned it into a system until the philosophical singer became the rigid dogmatist of anarchism, perhaps the greatest that Europe has today – certainly the most honest. I have become calmer, more sceptical, and am now more concerned with myself, with nurturing, maturing, and unfurling beautiful things within myself rather than with others, who nonetheless must find the right path within themselves. So we are asunder. But the gentle threads of dear memory bind us always.

He is famous now. Few heard the poet of 'Helene', *Storm* and the *Strong Year*[110]. But *The Anarchists* – circulated throughout world, translated into French by Louis de Hessem, translated into English by Georg Schumm and now appearing in cheap editions for the public – is known to all. It was angrily criticised and enthusiastically praised. Only no one has understood it the way the poet intended.

He is fat and conducts himself like a thin man. The impetuous, nervous haste of erratic, rapid gestures, his sudden, effervescent speech, do not accord with his broad, sedate body and plump shining cheeks. He has short legs and tends to push his heavy behind forward somewhat, so that he always seems to be blown from behind, about to fall on one. The words do not obey him fast enough. While speaking a sentence he thinks, and becomes entangled and stutters; he stutters with his hands and feet as well.

He laughs heartily when I ask him about antisemitism. His full, thick cheeks wobble. It strikes him as inadmissibly foolish and pitiable for people to argue about such things. 'Tell the antisemites that they are bad economists and generally asses. That is my opinion. Otherwise I do not know what else to say about this issue.'

'Now you know you cannot get off that easily. Antisemitism is after all …'

'But dear child, you cannot possibly demand that a serious person take antisemitism seriously. Anyone who continues to argue about religion or race, rather than positioning oneself as a person among people, convicts himself. Today there is only one question that supersedes

ANTISEMITISM

all others and decides everything: freedom or constraint. There is no other choice. He who desires liberty must, if he pursues his thoughts honestly and without fear, profess my anarchism, which disdains uproar and seeks only the peaceful reconciliation of all peoples.'

'You are simply an incorrigible utopian.'

'And you cannot think logically or maybe you do not wish to …'

'You should leave logic alone – it could do you harm. From those premises your entire anarchism can only arrive at its conclusion by a logical leap.'

'Prove it!'

'Easy! You start with liberty. As do I. I wish for the greatest liberty. But as long as another beside me is also free, it will always remain stunted, because my will is always inhibited and constrained by his. To be absolutely free I would have to be an absolute ruler. And so I arrive at Nietzsche and Barrès, and not you.'

'Only those who wish to be alone can be absolutely free.'

'So, if you yourself recognise that – but then your theory is already finished. If I cannot be absolutely free, only relatively so, then a little more or less matters not to me.'

'But you are forgetting that the higher the freedom of the individual, the higher the freedom of the other becomes.'

'Yes, if you could prove it, and if it were not just one of your empty assertions!'

'You always think solely of your condition of freedom, instead of thinking of it in general terms.'

'What do I care about the general public? If I am to change and improve, then I wish to do so radically. But you lot are strange. You want to do away with kings and priests and police because they irk you; but any old philistine, some idiot who is blind to art who disturbs me far more is free to remain. How do I get from the assertion of my liberty to the general liberty that you assert? That is the leap. It is the love of the people that is constantly invoked – but if I already love, then I do not need your revolution at all and will submit myself to any servitude.'

'It is not for love that I wish for general liberty, but because it promotes and secures my own liberty. I leave others alone so that I myself may be left alone. Of course, I must waive some of my desires. Of course, there will always be violence – no longer aggressive, but defensive. The condition of anarchy is not a flawless ideal, merely the best order of society in comparative terms. It cannot grant me the liberty to do anything I want. But it grants me the liberty not to do anything that I do not wish to do. I am not forced, and I must not force others …'

'Except to anarchism –'

'Not at all. I reject all violence. We need to make violence impossible; we do not achieve that by countering it with violence – the Devil cannot be driven out by Beelzebub. Passive resistance to aggressive violence is the only way to break it. I am not at all concerned with dynamite and bombs. I wait patiently, in the unshakeable conviction that liberty is the goal of natural development. There is no other route to it but that of calm, tireless, certain enlightenment, and of the example one offers,

ANTISEMITISM

until everyone understands the general advantage and no one wishes to be a slave to his slaves any longer.'

'Not all anarchists are so peaceful –'

'What people in Germany call anarchists are in fact dynamitists or communists – our worst enemies.'

'But where else do you aim to find followers?'

'In Paris, the *Autonomie individuelle*[111] movement is growing, and in America a small but steady and confident band of excellent men has been at work for years – Tucker in Boston, who owns *Liberty*[112], is their leader. I have come to regard Europe as a dying land … and even Germany, dear God! The Germans are always last in culture, but the first in any universal stupidity – like antisemitism. I have given up looking for reasonable people here.'

WILHELM FOERSTER

They say that Privy Councillor Foerster, the director of the Berlin Observatory[113], is one of the greatest astronomers, they praise his *Studies of Astrometry*.[114] My interest pertains to his leadership of the Berlin 'Ethical Society'[115], which is winning new disciples every day. Here I should like to repeat what I said about Egidy recently.

He sent me this avowal:

'Antisemitic ranting and hyperbole trespass mainly by the undiscriminating way that they insult and oppress the innocent and the culprit at the same time.

A cure for the diseased judgment of the crowd, however, is not to be sought in condemnatory words, but by healing the increasingly intolerable conditions of working life and of money-making. Jews are by no means solely responsible for these conditions, but in the Germanic and Slavic countries they have a highly significant share in the distress and suffering that arises as a result.

So it is incumbent on the volitional and intellectual power of the many noble-minded Jews in particular to cooperate vigorously in the rational transformation of our economic conditions.

It is gratifying to see how many have understood this and are working towards it.

Berlin, 9 May 1893.
W. Foerster.'

ALFRED NAQUET

I commenced the French series of my interviews with Alfred Naquet because, first of all, I wanted to quickly gain information about the current state of the issue in France, how it appears from every side, to supporters and foes alike, that I may be all the more knowledgeable and skilful in my study of the others. No one could offer this more clearly, more thoroughly and more fairly than the little Jew and great leader of the Boulangists[116] who, more than any other party, have struck antisemitism into the hearts of the mob. I am not here to hear him parroting the words of the well-meaning liberals, who simply wish to deny a movement that does not suit them, nor can he approve of rabble-rousing without expecting difficult questions from me, but rather I want him to honestly share the prevailing opinion of the people. It was also partly my curious old psychological penchant for a truly bizarre thinker, who always defended the most tender matters of sentiment with the most quibbling mind. And finally, it aroused my dramatic sentiment, because every author must gratefully honour the father of *Divorce*[117], which has provided so many new twists and forms to vaudeville …

I am summoned just in time because he is leaving Paris today to go on a quest to the south. Pretty maids with white caps are heading to market. In the shops they are scrubbing. Girls are humming their way home, with carnations in their rosy mouths like a still-sweet memory of night, like a last kiss on tired lips. So I walk, across Opéra, to Batignolles, where there are many streets of foreign cities, the rue de Berlin, de Londres, d'Amsterdam, d'Athènes.

Rue de Moscou, 44. Right at the top on the fifth floor of the lean, silent building. I am led into a narrow, bright, quiet room; his portrait by Alphonse Hirsch, which shows the strange mixture of pain and intellect in his tortured features, many books and heavy armchairs, cushions, chaise longues, which lend the room a faint morbidity as though it were home to one who wished to reflect in solitude and recover from suffering.

He is small, crooked and stooped. The severity of his abrupt and forceful profile under his smooth, white hair, behind his curly white beard, is softened by the agility of twitching lines, immediately registering the slightest change of mind. He speaks in fluent, clear, sure, print-ready sentences.

'The question does not hold the same significance for us that it does for you. For two reasons! First, because the number of Jews is far smaller – only about 70,000 all told; and also because they were emancipated much earlier – the Portuguese, of whom I am one, even before the

Revolution, the Alsatians and Germans during it, so all of them at least a hundred years ago. Of course, their assimilation has already progressed much further today than it has with you, where there was no emancipation until 1848[118]. Nevertheless, even we retain an atavistic hatred in the minds of our people, which a clever and ruthless faction is now trying to use for its own ends – the Jesuit faction. By that I do not at all mean the Catholic party in general; for now one must take care to separate the policies of the Jesuits from those of the Pope, who seems very enlightened, moderate and tolerant, with modern views. But the Jesuits, the implacable enemies of our revolutionary progress, hope that by fomenting hatred of the Jews they will once again seize the mob which they are now powerless to gain through other means. If they were to honestly announce their true intentions with their old religious slogans, their beleaguered faith and the cross, no one would listen to them any more. So they hide their wishes and their plans behind speeches that are more pleasing to the masses, and invoke hatred and envy against the Jews. But for them a Jew is anyone who is not a militant Catholic (*catholique militant*). Freethinkers, atheists, Protestants – anyone they do not care for they call a Jew, and although they term it an antisemitic movement, all they essentially desire is a clerical movement. These are the leaders who are joined by a few anxious capitalists who expect antisemitism to be a highly enjoyable 'diversion' of socialism – they wish to shut the proletariat's mouth with Jewish money. All these experiments have no chance in the provinces – there they know the Jews to be honest, diligent, industrious people, and there is no flagrant wealth there. Only in Paris, where a certain number of Jewish speculators have acquired large fortunes rapidly and not always fastidiously, were they able to gain a following, but they remained without power, without success. They have yet to put a single candidate into parliament – do not be deceived by the bluster from the *Libre Parole*[119]. There are a few people who are amused by antisemitic hatred – one cannot talk of a serious faction.'

'So you do not believe antisemitism has a future in France?'

'No ... nor anywhere else, even where antisemitism may actually have a rightful claim. I can well believe that the Jews in Romania and Russia are a miserable, mean people, as one often hears, and I myself recall from my childhood – I am now fifty-eight years old – even older Jews from before the emancipation, who were quite strange and alien. But does that not actually supply the best argument for emancipation? What is it that makes them so abject and miserable, if not precisely that bondage in which they are so deliberately held? Any race that one despises will eventually become despicable, and there is only one way to improve it – according it full freedom and full honour ...'

'Just one more question: the Boulangists to whom you belong, or at least once belonged, are they not considered antisemites?'

'In 1888, Boulangism began as an exclusively political party which was concerned with revision, with all sorts of constitutional issues and not a single word about antisemitism, which arose only timorously. It was not until the elections of 1889 that Drumont[120] and his men tried to win the party over to antisemitism, which they extolled as a highly effective and convenient means of agitation, and at that time Laur[121] did in fact hold an antisemitic conference. These were the beginnings of an antisemitic strain in the party, against which I immediately and decisively protested, as did the General, who wished to have nothing to do with antisemitism and struck all the antisemites from the list. As long as he was alive, the Boulangist party was never antisemitic and if he had had his way would never have become so. After his death, of course, and after the dissolution of the Comité, there was a growing alignment with the *Libre Parole*, not out of belief in its doctrine, but because they believed any means of stoking the passions of the people, proclaiming rebellion, promoting subversion was justified ... Which is why some of the socialists hold with the antisemites. They think: this may well be a Jesuit undertaking – we shall deal with them afterwards. Just as the Jesuits think: they may be revolutionaries – we shall deal with them afterwards ... Yes, they're a funny old mix, the antisemitic faction!'

JULES SIMON

Opposite the broad, solemn temple of the Madeleine, where you find the great flower market, and a deep, heavy, rapturous scent of yellow roses, brown lilacs and bloody carnations. The tall, lean house that shyly turns away from the square into a corner is most academically inclined; on the second floor lives the rotund, merry Meilhac[122], the father of *La Grande-Duchesse de Gérolstein* and *La belle Hélène*, who incidentally also wrote *Margot*, the daintiest comedy of the elegant life; on the fourth lives the venerable Jules Simon. For over forty years he has lived here, at the top, under the roof, in a delightful, colourful jostle of books, writings and papers piled up to the ceiling with barely a tiny patch free for a faded etching, some slender bronzes and pictures of old friends.

He lies in a broad, comfortable chair, his mighty, bald, yellow skull in repose, his heavy, thick eyelids closed as though he were dozing, with a mild, placatory smile playing about his pained, acerbic mouth. With the English character of his broad, bulky, well-groomed countenance he slightly resembles Gneist[123], who like him has something of the retiree, the pensioner. But his sharp, strong beak of a nose and cunning little eyes lend him a mocking, sarcastic, satirical air that has nothing of the stiff dignity of the German pedant. In his speech there is a whimsical mix of warmth, which excuses everything and assumes the best, of quiet mockery, which fails to conceal human misery, and of a sad patience which has renounced a host of hopes; and he chirrups with a thin, furtive, girlish voice that begins in shrill tones then falls breathlessly and extinguishes in darkness. Everything about him is gentle and kind, and he appears veiled in the mellow spirit of a life that has always been composed of order, peace and moderation. Ernest Daudet once expressed it in a single sentence: *Ce fut surtout et avant tout un libéral et un modéré.*[124] So he was as a young and eloquent teacher at the École Normale and the Sorbonne; so he was as he stood in the Constituante[125] of 1849; so he was as he fought against the tempestuous ultramontanism of Montalembert[126]; so he was when he refused the oath to the government of the coup d'état; so he was when he quarrelled with the communists as Minister of National Defence from the fall of the Emperor to the fall of Thiers; so he has receded with dignity before the raw passion of MacMahon[127] – brave, just, prudent, free and restrained.

He receives me with kind, sweet words, praising Vienna and the Viennese; he visited some years ago and remembers the hospitable city with gratitude.

I put to him my request that he enlighten me

about antisemitism in France.

'My God, the antisemites! That is a most murky and confused faction of many incompatible elements. Just like it used to be with Boulangism, which was also promoted by all sorts of parties – and so you had Rochefort standing alongside the Princess d'Uzès[128]! And now we have antisemitism bringing together the old atheist Cluseret[129] alongside the devout Drumont. Reactionaries and revolutionaries all mixed up together. All enemies of the Republic together. First, there is the Church. It has the vocation, so to speak, of opposing the Jews, and the Catholics were antisemites before antisem- itism, *avant la lettre*, before it made tawdry concessions to the mob, before it even became a popular formula. They are the Princess d'Uzès of antisemitism. Then come the socialists, who are highly sought-after, because one senses the weakness of religious arguments, which are no longer effective today. The alliance between the two enemies may seem strange, but it is quite natural. The reactionaries tell themselves: we need socialist assistance to rule the mob. And the socialists say: we approve of anything that encourages dissatisfaction, confusion, uproar; then we shall see. They are not particular in their choice of means. That is the modern way now. The only aim is to strike your opponent! No one asks about truth or justice. Anything that might work is welcome. Any weapon against the enemy is valid. I have experienced that myself. People did not hesitate to call me a Jew even though I am not and never have been – my sister has even dedicated herself to missionary work and founded seven churches in South America. But that does not matter at all to these people. Anyone they do not like they call Jew. There really is nothing more to it – I merely mention this to demonstrate the nature of their combat, the *légèreté* of their claims and all their evidence … First, the Catholics who follow the old ancestral, instinctive hatred of the Jews; second, the revolutionaries who hate all order; supported by the great mass of malcontents who are beguiled by every new catchphrase. Little wonder that there is so much commotion in the streets – but one can hardly speak of a serious movement. Real people do not listen to them and do not care for their agitation. There is no antipathy to the Jews … or at most only some of the Jews, against the Alsatians and Germans … and not because of their religion. One must differentiate with care. There is no hatred for the Portuguese Jews. This I know from Bordeaux, for example, where I was once elected. There are many Jews there. They are in trade, in banking, in industry; they are valued for their diligence and zeal and they enjoy a great deal of respect and honour. They are also quite like the Catholic French. Not like Alsace. Things are entirely different there – something with which I am somewhat familiar as I have long-standing close relations with Mulhouse. There they hate the Jews and that is how antisemitism came to us, from Alsace. Alsatians brought it to Paris and here some circles are now very sensitive to the Alsatian, or rather the German Jews. Especially on the stock market. I remember – it may have been about two years ago – a case where a protégé of the Rothschilds failed in his attempt to become an *agent de change*, despite patronage; the syndicate simply refused to admit him and said, we already have enough

Jews. But these are only ever individual cases. Otherwise the Jews cannot complain. We even had two Jewish ministers during the empire, and we have Jewish divisional generals, and I do not believe anything will bring change to the social standing of the Jews. I do not believe that antisemitism has a future here. It is too contrary to the spirit of our race, which has always been tolerant and liberal. We are a *pays de tolérance, même d'indifferénce*[130]. One should not be deceived by a little noise.'

ANATOLE LEROY-BEAULIEU

There are two brothers, Anatole and Paul, with only one year between them, both economists – probably the greatest present-day France has to offer – and both teachers at the École libre des sciences politiques[131], both in the Académie des sciences morales[132]. Paul, who is also the founder of the *Economiste français*[133], has written about administration in England and France, about the doctrine of taxes as well as a criticism of the socialists, *Le collectivisme*; Anatole on the Second Empire and Russian studies in the three volumes of *The Empire of the Tsars and the Russians* which made his name. Both of them are much engaged in journalism, with the elder a faithful worker at the *Revue des Deux Mondes* and Paul a diligent contributor to *Temps*, *Débats*, and *Revue contemporaine*.

Now Anatole lives in the countryside and only comes in for Saturday sessions of the Academy. He summons me there so we might converse in comfort afterwards. And so I set out – the things one does when ambition is piqued, for one's profession and the sake of one's brothers! I wander over the narrow bridge from the quay, happily taking in the bright images proffered by the majestic current, toward the Corinthian order of the solemn institute founded by Mazarin[134]. There is a severe, dignified calm all about, as though the vast square were ruefully atoning for its criminal history; for here once stood the Hôtel de Nesle, where the sultry Margaret of Burgundy, wife of the tenth Louis, enticed young strangers for her wild, lustful purposes and then, once the tumult of precipitous pleasures had passed, killed them and cast them into the Seine, lurking darkly below.

My footsteps echo. First I go searching a little through the marble, past pale busts of stern thinkers, until at last I find a servant who drowsily scrutinises the guest and sullenly admits me into the session. It is a long, narrow, deep hall, the high walls green, green also the solemn tables, with busts in the niches and a powerful portrait of the scarlet cardinal. But to look upon these academics is to imagine oneself at the opera – bald heads, nothing but bald heads, bare, yellow, steep, pointed, wrinkled pates in highly picturesque shapes. All the limp heads are bowed down, blinking and tired and smiling softly and gently, as though in a dream, while the speaker mutters furtively from his papers. The mood would be conducive to writing Sleeping Beauty[135].

Paul Leroy-Beaulieu is chairing the meeting. He is tall, strong, handsome, with noble features, luxuriant curls barely a-shimmer with first grey, gallantry and verve in every gesture. Beside him Anatole seems paler and gentler, with a quiet, fine, morbid expression, blurred, withered and wizened by the patience of long labour.

Once the last of the assembled has finally murmured his report, and the tired, crooked men have slowly departed in stiff, black coats with sharp, grave collars, we sit down and talk.

'It goes without saying that I am an opponent of antisemitism. I oppose it as a Christian and a Frenchman. As a Christian, I cannot tolerate a doctrine that proclaims hatred and sows discord among men. As a Frenchman, I cannot disavow our ancient tradition of justice and freedom, which gives us our historical position in Europe. Antisemitism goes against the spirit of our race. It came to us from abroad, from the other side of the Rhine, and shall not find a home here. We shall never see ourselves reflected in a political doctrine that is a wild mixture of reactionary instincts and revolutionary desires. On no account do I seek to deny that there is some truth to be found in the complaints of the antisemites. They are right to complain about the idolatry of gold, the shameful corruption of governments and the exploitation of the people. But it is in locating the cause of the evil that they err. It lies much deeper than they think, and if all the Jews were to be expelled from France, from Europe even, the vices from which we suffer would remain the same. The solution is not as easy as they think, and antisemitism, which holds Jews to be guilty of everything, will only delay the cure that must come from within ourselves … That, more or less, is how I would profess my views on antisemitism.'

'Do you consider antisemitism – in France – to be a religious or a nationalist cause?'

'I think there are numerous factors at once. But

the national and social factors are probably the more important. The religious factor is of little significance. It is there, and people accuse the Jews of de-Christianizing society without reflecting that they *déjudaïsent* themselves at the same time, because both Aryans and Semites are experiencing the same paganisation of modern development which triumphs over Torah and Gospels alike. But it is only a very small group that is guided by such concerns. Religious issues no longer retain their power over us, and were antisemitism not supported by nationalist and social instincts, it would hold no danger. It is the national aspect that lends it significance, and it is as a form of protectionism aiming to defend the culture of the fatherland against foreign elements that it has won the most allies. It is understandable in this time of national conceit that one might not care to tolerate a separate people within the people, a state to itself within the state, as is claimed of the Jews. There is absolutely no evidence for this claim, and no validity to the comparison with the Chinese in America so favoured by the antisemites. Since emancipation the Jews have been just as fine Frenchmen as their Catholic and Protestant brothers; for nationality is no longer decided by race but by a community of the mind, by customs, by sentiment. The German manner of determining nationality by race seems, to our French custom, just as foolish and reactionary as the Russian manner of determining it by uniformity of religion. This is simply not possible for modern peoples which have evolved throughout history, because they are all conglomerates. On what race should we base our French nationality, composite of Cimbri, Gauls, Iberians and

Latins that we are? And there is nothing to support the belief that we are pure Aryans, as one cannot forget the effect of the fossil European races. And just think of the Ligurians in Spain and Provence! Think of the Finns in Hungary and Russia! For where in Europe today is there a race that has remained unalloyed and pure, that is Aryan beyond all doubt? But if one acknowledges the impossibility of determining nationality by race and bases it instead on unity of history and development, exclusion of the Jew is unjust and foolish in equal measure; some of them – the Provençal, for example – have been settled in our country for two thousand years. They are as much a part of our people as the others whom they resemble in all things. Of course you cannot claim that of everyone. Especially not of the Polish and German Jews who come to us from Frankfurt and Galicia and are often an egregious element in business. But it is not because they are Jews, but rather because they are Germans or Poles, that we perceive them as strangers.'

'Do you think antisemitism has a future in France?'

'I do not believe it has a future, but I believe it will last long enough because it is convenient for the socialists. There is much more socialism in it than one might think, and it will go on becoming more socialist, because we have so few Jews that the movement will soon turn against property, against capital in general of its own accord, with no concern for denomination or race. Today they say: all Jews are thieves. Tomorrow they will say: all bourgeois are thieves. The Jew is merely a convenient expression of their agitation against the entire bourgeoisie, and it seems inevitable to me that antisemitism will become increasingly revolutionary in its opposition to the state order. The conservative elements are disappearing – only a few remain on the extreme right, such as the Comte de Mun, while Drumont already treats the Comte de Paris[136] as a friend and companion to the Jews. Before long 'Jew' will be nothing more than a convenient word for property in general, for the rich. Before long antisemitism will be subsumed entire into pure socialism. That strikes me as inexorable, and it strikes me that this is its true danger. It is not so much the Jews that it threatens as the bourgeois order as a whole. We should not deny that it does broach some things about the Jews that really are unappealing, and it may even be highly useful to them, by drawing their own attention to these things. For example, the major role they play in Freemasonry, often less by conviction than as a means of advancing in society, of gaining connections and penetrating otherwise closed circles, is indeed disconcerting. But even if one were inclined to believe that a calm discussion of these matters cannot harm the Jew, it is impossible to overlook the danger that in the end this will merely delay, complicate or even annul their assimilation. Here I should like to bring your attention to my book on antisemitism[137] in which I tell of a Russian Jew, a student, who told me: "If we are persistently treated as a foreign people, why would we not then consider truly becoming one? We strive to leave our particularity behind and are forcibly returned to it. Would it really be surprising if our pride were to retaliate and we sought to resurrect ancient Israel? And why should we not succeed in establishing a Jewish state where we may live according to our laws and customs, according to our traditions?" Thus it may in fact occur by dint of antisemitism that the Jews become what the antisemites of today falsely claim them to be – a separate people unto themselves among the peoples. That is why I fight antisemitism, as aware as I am of some Jewish faults, which usually lie in circumstances rather than race, and can be cured by rational reform. I am thinking particularly of Algiers, where complaints about the exploitation of the Arabs by Jewish usury, which naturally Christians practice often enough as well, are in fact not without foundation. One must provide legal protection for the small property holders. Different places call for different remedies. One cannot make the same laws for every country. But this wild agitation against a whole class of our citizens is contemptible and mean, unworthy of the age in which we live, and the nation to which we belong.'

ALPHONSE DAUDET

Daudet is a real Wandering Jew of lodgings. He moves constantly. Each novel is written in a different home, chosen according to his latest mood. He has made every corner of Paris his home at some point. But again and again he is irresistibly drawn to the Latin Quarter, to the Jardin du Luxembourg, where the enthusiastic young man once indulged sultry dreams, the audacious desires of young distress, beneath the squat, mean forms of the round towers of Saint-Sulpice which he viewed from his narrow, miserable, tumble-down mansard at the Grand Hotel du Sénat, at fifteen francs a month.

He now lives on rue de Bellechasse, a dark, silent, forlorn street that rises from quai d'Orsay, the wide, solemn square of the Academy, where the booksellers offer old black, crumbling folios; through the quarter, past the Cour des Comptes[138], which has been slumbering in sooty ruins since the Commune, shot through with the heavy green of long, dark, lush grass now sprouting there. To the rear courtyard. And then up three steep flights of stairs. I recall what Bardoux, the Fine Arts Minister of 1877, once said to an English emissary: 'You do not know Paris, my dear, and that is because you do not climb high enough when you go visiting. *La France n'habite pas au premier, la France loge au troisième étage, au quatrième, parfois sous les toits.*'[139]

A dark, austere, quiet room enrobed in dull, soft, tender, placatory colours with heavy drapes drawn against the world, against light and noise from without. An anxious, apprehensive, suspended mood, like the sick bed of a shy and sensitive woman. And all bathed in a deep, cloudy grey from which, beneath the bright image of Edmond de Goncourt by Bracquemond[140], the white pallor of his face shines spectral and tormented. Everything seems on the verge of fleeing, trickling away, and his features, his forms float in the mist, like a dream of a visitation from spirits. The famous portrait by Carrière[141] captures the mystical and disembodied essence of the nervous writer.

He is holding the crutch without which he can no longer move, and he squirms without cease, like a feverish patient turning the pillows over and vainly seeking relief from a thousand layers. The noble face, marked by suffering, bears an inexpressible refinement of lines and wrinkles; they speak of the habit of long torments, deep convulsions, a mild glimmer of that ultimate grace often seen in consumptive maidens. He seems ill, but he does not seem old; one would not suspect his 53 years. He seems more like a beautiful youth marked for death. And anyone alert to the strange contradiction of profound reverie in his veiled glances and the mockery of his harsh

ANTISEMITISM

lips will realise that he has always been a troubadour, a boulevardier.

He speaks softly and gently, but the words are warm and moist, shining and swelling with sentiment, ever thawing under that *sensibilité violente* which Lemaître[142] referred to as the dominant element of his works, of his life. He speaks nervously, shifting from one topic to another, without rigorous order, in ragged, rushing sentences.

'I am not a politician, I do not care for politics, I do not understand it – I imprudently follow my moods, and they are changeable. So – I do not know anything about the antisemitic doctrine; I cannot offer reasons for or against it. I can only speak for my moods, which may not always be just – I am merely the vassal of my nerves. Suddenly I will feel well-disposed for no reason, and for no reason I may become ill-disposed again. It is an odd thing with me and antisemitism. When I was still on close terms with Drumont I was a fierce opponent of the antisemites. Now that we no longer see each other – I do not know why it should be, but sometimes I feel that I am moving closer to his thinking. We were once very close. He would often come to see me, and each time we would argue about antisemitism. But we could never agree. I am unlucky enough to have very little religion – it does not interest me, or appeal to me. Perhaps that is a misfortune, but it is one I cannot change. And to hate a person for his belief, to revile him, persecute him, that struck me as quite shameful and abominable. So we always quarrelled; and my wife especially, who is just and gentle, would became quite agitated. Now we no longer see each other. He is an outstanding person and a writer of unusual importance, but passionate, unjust and entirely immoderate. The things he says about me now! The fact that he says I may have talent, but then utters the most ghastly things about my greed and my ungovernable urge to amass money ... that I married off my son to the Hugo girl[143] to enrich myself ... as if sons could be married off so easily ... and I ask you, what does one see of one's daughter-in-law's money? But that is just how he is. Yes – what was I saying? At that time I was a fierce opponent of the antisemites. But now – I cannot deny that now and then I catch myself thinking strange thoughts. If you look at the great swindles and fiddles, and when you realise that in all those dirty dealings the Jews always play the leading role – well, ultimately it becomes difficult to avoid a certain antipathy. This does not prevent me maintaining friendships with numerous Jews. But in the depths of my soul I have become slightly suspicious. If antisemitism were to triumph, I would be the first to protest against it ... because it is unacceptable, and it could endanger our culture. But as long as the Jews prevail and run all the major businesses and the entirety of politics, I feel *vaguement* antisemitic. For example: I used to live in the old Hôtel Richelieu on the place des Vosges. It was the only building on the whole square that was not yet owned by the Jews. Now, there is nothing one can actually say against that. But I cannot help it, I must confess that it gives me an unpleasant feeling. I am not a specialist in the matter; I do not much distinguish between Portuguese and German Jews, like the connoisseurs of Jewry; naturally I condemn agitation against the

Jews; I recognise the dangers that antisemitism holds for order and freedom – but I would be lying if I were to deny a certain slight, vague aversion that sometimes stirs within me.'

'What do others in your circles think about the issue ... the writers and artists?'

'I do not believe that there is any antisemitism there. I have never found a trace. But I have to say it is very difficult to judge – how would it manifest itself?'

'I mean in the Société des gens de lettres[144], for example. Has there been an antisemitic strain apparent there?'

'No, never – not that it would prove anything in any case. The Société des gens de lettres has no significance. You should not believe that because Zola is now president – he would be president anywhere now. There is no association whose president he does not wish to be: fire brigade, janitors, nightwatchmen – since he has acquired his new academic mind, it is all the same to him. *Il adore la présidence* ... But no, I do not believe that antisemitism exists in our circles. Some of the younger writers have depicted what goes on in the Jewish world, as Lavedan does in *Prince d'Aurec*[145]. But then I did that twelve years ago, in *Rois en exil*, which was created out of a strong feeling for the power of money. At the time I was booed and hissed, because both the Jews and the swank aristocrats were appalled by the play ... And by the way, I am not at all a theatre person, either.'

'You are writing a new play for next season?'

'Yes, I am creating a drama and a novel from the same material. It is entitled *Le soutien de famille*[146]. The title is ironic – a pillar of the family who has breakfast brought to him in bed at 11 am, something like that. The novel takes a very bitter, harsh turn. For the stage, of course, I have to smooth it out a little and soften it, because everything there must always have a taste of *féerie*, so to speak.'

FRANCIS MAGNARD

The editor of *Le Figaro* has served in journalism from the bottom up. He got his start with all sorts of satirical weeklies and youthful revues. Barely 25, he began working for the newspapers of Mr Villemessant, as editor of *L'Événement* and *Le Figaro*. He functioned as the '*liseur*', combing the newspapers every day for the latest Parisian opinion and offering it to the masses in handy, convenient formulae. In 1876 he became editor-in-chief, and after the death of Villemessant, one of the three directors of *Le Figaro*, which he transformed from a stuffy plaything of the monarchical and clerical faction to a free platform for all the new whims, whimsies and fashions that come and go among the people.

His literary baggage is light: a novel, *L'Abbé Jérôme*, published in 1869 and now unavailable, and the satirical work *Vie et aventures d'un positiviste, histoire paradoxale* (1876). It may however suffice for the Academy[147], for which he is now standing for the first time, against his will no less. It is not the writer it will receive, but the master of the new journalism.

It is not easy to arrive at a proper judgment of one who has so many enemies with frustrated ambitions, so many friends bribed with benefits, each according to the services he denies or grants. Some praise him as an incomparable explorer constantly drawing fresh talent from its blithe concealment, saying that he is wondrously equipped with a sensitive, unerring, fine nose for the slightest impulses in art, in life, in political processes, and they praise the delectable clarity of those tiny little articles which every morning, in a few short, spare lines, provide the formula for the day, the spirit of the moment, thus happily proving Villemessant's maxim: *Donner tous les jours une idée aux lecteurs.*[148] Others revile his tendency to defend today what he repudiated yesterday, without conviction, without loyalty to people or issues, without true consequence to his plans, and say he may be the first to discover you but will also be the first to betray you; they revile too his soft, supple, selfless style, which always bears the traces of his most recent encounter, the last thing he read, and has nothing but the vapid, repellent clarity of shallow waters. And thus praise and contumely alternate. And if that sweet, delightful poet Catulle Mendès calls him one of the *esprits les plus intéressants et les plus intéressés de ce temps*[149], the mocking Bergerat called him an *equilibriste moral, social, artistique,* who is able to do one thing only: *satisfaire toutes les opinions, contenter tous les partis, tirer de l'abonnement dans tous les camps.*[150]

They are probably both right, the enthusiast and the detractor, and probably they both mean the same thing, each eyeing it differently as it helps or hinders him. He is not a politician; he has no insight of his own, no *vision particulière* of things that might drive him to passionate organisation of the affairs of state. He is not an artist because he is entirely lacking in specific sensibility. He is not a stylist with his own personal form of events. He is a philistine; he has all the common instincts of the mob. He is a snob; he has all the passing fashions of the boulevard. But he understands the instincts that the mob merely senses, and discovers the fashions that the boulevard then copies from him. He is always a snob or philistine in a form that others will only assume six months hence. He hears desires not yet sounded in others; he has the fashions before they become modern; and half a year earlier than anyone else he always senses the change in mood. He is simply the great journalist who must resemble the multitude to act upon it, to rule over it, but must also sense any stirring before it so that he might guide it.

He is short, nimble and sharp. Sharp – that is the word that best expresses his nature. Sharp the short, narrow, white beard that frames his narrow, smart, sharp face, and sharp the quick and agile gestures that he thrusts at you like whirring daggers. And in the cramped room whose space is monopolised by an immense table he ceaselessly paces like a fox in a cage, constantly turning and circling in wide arcs. He is highly hospitable, with that light, swift, devoted courtesy of the Parisians, who adopt every human being in this miserable life as a colleague; but in the breathless man's rash haste, in his nervous, twitching expressions, one senses the pressing burden of concerns and dealings. There is a near mercantile zeal to his speech and gestures, the urgency of great entrepreneurs, like the traders at the stock exchange, along with that supple, succinct intimacy that speaks of familiarity with many.

He speaks the way one telegraphs – just the phrases, with the addressee left to establish the conjunctions. This may well be how he dictates the essence of a 'lead', leaving an assistant to augment it and provide rhetorical polish. It is a strange blend of hard and gentle, because he wishes to say so many things with a single word, to say everything at once, and yet he does not wish to omit even one of his thousandfold preoccupations.

'Antisemitism is an invention of Mr Édouard Drumont – by which I mean, of course there has always been anti-Jewish sentiment, prejudice and hatred, but it was only ever a purely personal matter. You liked the Jews, or you did not, as you saw fit – it had nothing to do with politics. It was Drumont who first created, discovered political antisemitism, and it was only with *La France Juive*[151] that it came to life. Drumont turned his individual antipathy into a general principle which, however, was soon denied by its own author and underwent numerous changes. Created initially out of his own religious sentiments, it presented itself as a racial question and now as a social question; reactionary to begin with, it becomes more revolutionary with every passing day, and the good Drumont, who is passionate, immoderate, yet gallant and honourable, will again take fright from the consequences of his actions. It began in opposition to Jewish money, but will turn on Christian money before long. He has already lost that touch that betrayed his origins as a religious writer, and the agitation against Jewish profit is becoming ever more distinctly agitation against any form of profit not gained through labour. It is only a matter of time, a few months maybe, until these transformations cease and pure antisemitism becomes a diversion of high society at most, and pure socialism supplants it. There is no doubt in my mind.'

'Do you think that they will pass laws against the Jews?'

'My God! I do not care to play the prophet. One can so easily make a fool of oneself.'

'I merely mean, do you think laws against the Jews, exceptional laws that violate general law, are even possible?'

'Possible! Ultimately anything is possible here, and one should never say that something will not come to be. It would not be the first time that we experience today what seemed fantastically mad and impossible yesterday. But of course – one might say that as long as today's bourgeois order prevails, laws against the Jews are not possible. It would require a revolution in all things and the end of the modern state. As long as things remain legal and normal, it is not possible. It would require the chaotic collapse of conditions as a whole. But I do not think this is what the antisemites are aiming for. For them it is not about such laws at all. They wish to create a hostile mood against the Jews – that is all. They are not calling for laws. This is most likely because France lacks that Jewish usury which stokes such desires in other countries. Here the Jews are in the large companies, they are not involved in petty usury – except in Algiers, where there is certainly a growing, pressing need for protection against the terrible exploitation. Here it is different. Here we do not know the Jews as usurers. And that is precisely why I believe that antisemitic agitation has no future, that it only advances the socialist cause. That, to me, is the danger. And that is why I would always fight against it; that is why I would persistently and heedlessly combat it, even if – and this I thoroughly contest – they were right in their theories about the Jews, because I feel they imperil things that have nothing to do with the Jews, that is, all the conditions of the modern state and the entire form of our current political progress. And anyway, its initial strength and force are already exhausted. It was three or four years ago that it truly aroused serious concern. Now its power, its validity is already falling considerably, and soon it will disappear like a horrible nightmare.'

ARTHUR MEYER

The house of *Le Gaulois*, led by the handsome Arthur Meyer, is at 2 rue Drouot, a few steps away from the noise of the boulevards, before one comes to the graceful, bright *Figaro* manor. Rush and bustle all around, a constant back and forth, up and down, down the hall and up the narrow winding staircase. It is not easy slipping into the maelstrom and tumult of the hot, noisy, bright Salle des Dépêches[152].

This *salle* is a speciality of French newspapers. They are on far more intimate terms with the reader than our newspapers. For us it is enough that we supply him with reports and opinions; the currency, breadth and accuracy of the reports, the finest thinking we can find and, if you are lucky, a pleasing form – we do not believe we owe him any more than that. But here they seek to take care of all his business, all his concerns, to facilitate every desire. They wish to become assistants in the life of the reader. They wish to manage everything for him. Their aim is that he should seek advice and assistance from them for every question, every quandary, every need. And so they lure him to them, to the editorial office, where each seeks settlement of his concerns, his complaints, where each brings the latest rumours from the street, the latest sentiments of the mob, so that they might receive the narrative of the now, the events of the day in person without delay. An exchange from which both profit.

They need some means to attract him. One is the Salle des Dépêches. That is the name for a large room, open to the street, with numerous counters, where you can subscribe to the paper, order editions, make enquiries, conduct your correspondence, telephone, telegraph, with any number of diversions such as the *théâtrophone*, phonograph, caricatures, with photographs, pictures and sketches showing every event of the day, the latest criminal and the latest minister, the preacher and the fashionable cocotte, canny gentlemen and pretty girls. There is much idle strolling and exchange of mocking jests. I love listening to them and gawking with them. There hangs van Dyck[153], now the great passion of every beauty; the victor Dodds[154]; and Le Roy, the revolutionaries' clownish candidate for the Academy, who proudly puffs out his Bolivian uniform between the ravaged, ragged face of Lisbonne and the thin, shaky, lean Tournadre[155]; there hangs tired, haggard, sad Daudet beside the imperious and brutal profile of Zola, and there hang the highlights of the salons and a curious assembly of Communards from 1871.

But now it is time to go upstairs. He has summoned me for five. And at six o'clock, at the 'green hour'[156], the pale sun of my nights will be awaiting me once more in Café Riche, next door.

The impetuous surge of guests cannot linger on the stairs. All around a crush of runners, messengers, reporters; political and journalistic renown passes before your eyes. Descending now is Mermeix with his malicious, stark, earthen expression that would so like to ape Girardin's Mephistophelian skull, and I meet the lively, graceful and elegant Marcel Hirsch[157], the beloved Benjamin of the Parisian press, who two years ago attended the Salzburg Mozart jubilee and immediately won the hearts of all with his convivial grace ...

Arthur Meyer is a strange blend. First, the jobbing reporter, the kind you see in the caricatures – the easy, broad jobber who knows that he can do anything. Then again he has something of the *larbin*[158], the stately valet, who over time assumes the gestures, looks and affectations of his master. But even beneath that smooth, vain, hypocritical manner one cannot fail to recognise the 'good chap' who, as long as his conceit is not provoked, remains at heart agreeable, and the pained lines around the weary lips of the *viveur* reveal that he too has had his portion of woe. He speaks softly, mildly, courteously, but nervously and rashly – a curious hybrid of flirtatious baron and lisping entrepreneur.

I present my request. He inclines his dandified head, ponders a while in a pose that recalls a monument, and replies: 'The question is a little sensitive for me. I am a Jew and at the same time director of a highly Catholic paper. You understand that this is a somewhat delicate situation. I run the risk of saying something improper or banal. I must maintain my reserve.'

'I have come to you precisely because you are a Jew and a leader of Catholics, aristocrats. For us, to whom antisemitism appears primarily as a Catholic and reactionary movement ...'

A subtle smile indicates that he can view the interview from the other side, unwillingly, but he is kind enough to submit. 'One cannot claim that at all. One cannot claim that there is much antisemitism among the aristocracy, among the Catholics. Instead it seems to be a social movement. I do not believe it has much to do with religion or race. At most towards the German Jews perhaps – but the Spanish and French are not perceived as foreigners. Rather it is probably just a movement of hatred and envy against money, against finery, against the ruling classes in general – one calls them Jews when one means the rich. I also believe that its strength is already exhausted and its time has passed. By the way, as I said, these are my personal conjectures and thoughts, which are mine alone and not for public dispute. That is something I avoid entirely. By that I mean we Jews are best advised to keep out of it and can safely leave judgment to the chivalrous spirit of the nation. That is the attitude I have sketched out for myself and it seems to me the most prudent, even if I might have cause to regret it at this moment, because it robs me of the pleasure of fulfilling what you wish of me. And I am always happy to be of service to colleagues.'

ÉDOUARD PAILLERON

Édouard Pailleron, of the Academy, the delicate, subtle, only slightly precious conversationalist of *Le Monde où l'on s'ennuie*, *La Souris* and *L'Étincelle*[159], writes:

'Whether race against race or class against class or party against party – all wars are social wars, that is, struggles for existence.

Although the combatants may refine their means to deceive themselves about their cause, in the end they always hold the same objective: to take what they do not have from those that have it, or to defend what they have against those who do not.

"Antisemitism" and "socialism" are nothing but new banners in this eternal battle!'

SÉVERINE

You see her name every day. She writes in the *Figaro*, in the *Gaulois*, in the *Écho de Paris*, in the *Journal*. There are six, seven articles a week, sometimes more. She appears to be tireless. Only Henry Fouquier[160], perhaps, can compare.

It is something that comes only to those possessed of rich, sure knowledge and broad, communicable experience, with that nimble obedience of form which observes every sign, which always and immediately strikes the right tone. It cannot be subject to a mood that changes unpredictably. It must not issue from a surge of emotions that may stagnate and fail without warning. It must not stick to the passion that is a stranger to regulation. Its means are order of the mind, abundance of memory and a willing, ever cheerful technique. This is an old law of the prolific writer.

So one may expect to find in her a wise, mature, experienced woman who has established a lithe and subservient style for herself. But one encounters something quite different. She creates not from intellect, from experience, in fixed forms and ready templates. Instead, her pen goes where it may, carelessly, driven by feeling and emotion. Every word is perceived as a gift of creative delight, as an offering of passion, enthusiasm and intoxication.

It is odd. What she creates can only emerge under the spell of strange, rare, special, thrilling charms. But to deliver her copy punctually every day, she must be able to summon such stimuli at any time. She compels enthusiasm, passion and intoxication. She commands her moods. She gushes precisely from five to nine every day. Stirrings and fevers arrive dutifully as she sets them in her articles. How does she do it? Where did she obtain such an agreeable, useful, biddable demon? It must be a persistent urge of unusual dimensions. It must be an inexhaustible and tenacious stimulus, constantly renewed by things as they are, the sting of an insatiable desire that grows daily from renunciation. It must be an in-born, inflexible indignation in her nature.

It is the indignation of a feminine soul against the male order of this world. She talks and argues with men about the plans and precepts of the state. But she negotiates as a woman who is only ever a woman, womanly in every fibre of her thoughts and feelings. She expresses her femininity, offended by the male spirit in all things. This is her secret. This is what is new in her. This is what makes her incomparable. Often enough we have seen women who zealously acquire male minds, a masculine attitude to all matters, and a masculine attitude to every task until they are able to compete. But she is the first to consistently, courageously profess the feminine sensibility of things and the feminine dream of a just world replete with beauty and morality, against the rule of power and coercion.

In assessing values for their utility or futility she only ever consults her feminine sentiment. She eschews reason if it should fail to bring beauty, joy and serenity, refusing to accept it or hear evidence for the necessity of evils. Whatever offends a single person on earth offends her, and what offends her must not be. Her only criticism: but it hurts! Her only argument: but it will help! Sincere, audacious femininity devoid of moderation or modesty – such is her talent.

Hence the revolutionary sentiment that has always driven her to the poor, driven her to oppose the powerful and the rich, because the plight of the people pains her, like an ugly, dull shade that must be removed, like a harsh din that distresses the nerves. Hence her gentle, heartfelt sympathies for anarchists and nihilists, who appeal to her romantic nature. Hence her scornful rage against the agents of Marxism who seek power where she wishes to help. Hence amid all the pious, passionate gravity there is always a delicate, mischievous, subtle grace, because even in the most intense mêlée of emotions she does not forget the mirror. Hence the carefree politics of her own devising, which she once humorously called *l'école buissonnière de la Révolution*[161]. Hence the curious state of affairs that she cannot get along with any party and is loved by all, that she writes for the revolutionaries and for the reactionaries, and that she is a friend of Louise Michel[162] and the Princess of Monaco.

She is inexhaustible and readily remains so as every day brings her something new – the feminine response to every event. And she remains so amid the thousands of fast and fiery monologues of which some – too few, too modest! – are collected in a lovely, wonderful book, *Pages rouges*, dedicated to the memory of her great friend, the implacable Jules Vallès[163]; so she is always effortlessly different from the others, with a strange, new taste, and yet in her tireless charity, in her invincible assistance, in her inscrutable love, she is always the same, a Saint Elizabeth of the boulevards, advancing through the supplicant crowd with her generous bounty of consoling words and pious works.

Her life is quickly told, because there is more soul than story to it. Her good, industrious father worked for the prefect of the police, revering the government and fearing his superiors, a minor official who worked his way up, patiently endeavouring for years to reach each new position. And so the daydreaming Miss Remy grew up in bourgeois tranquillity, married a Mr Rheïne[164], soon divorced, returned to her parents and became a pupil of the impetuous communist Vallès whom she honoured with rapturous devotion, remaining by his side until his death. Her second husband, Doctor Guébhard[165] of the Institute, provided the funds for her to establish the *Cri du peuple*[166], which bore her name until 1888 – but in the long run she could not hold with the scholars of socialism; she hated any school that offered the people dogma in place of bread, and hated the hatred that they profess in place of eternal love, and perhaps did not suit a newspaper at all because she respects all opinions and listens placably to her opponent. Now she is in a state of vagabondage – interviewing for *Figaro*, reviewing theatre in the *Jour*, agitating on behalf of the poor in the *Gaulois*, and soliciting mercy in the *Matin*, in the *Eclair*, in *Gil Blas*, in the *Écho de Paris*, in the *Journal*. That is her element – helping, always helping, helping everyone; the little telegraphists on a hunger strike and the pitmen of Saint-Étienne, for whom she collected sixty thousand francs, and old Élise Duguéret, the forgotten tragedienne, and good Mother Jouault, provisioner for the shooters of Châteaudun, and the murderer Padlewski[167], whom she hid from the bailiffs and ushered safely over the border with the help of her friend, journalist Georges de Labruyère. She always finds time for consolation and assistance, with time left over to be the loveliest woman with the prettiest ideas, like coming up with the title for *La Cocarde* and the red carnation of the Boulangists[168].

She always has time, because she lives in immutable order maintained with rigour and precision – that is the secret of the Parisians, which explains their wonders of labour and pleasure. She sleeps until eleven, bathes and then devotes herself to matters of beauty, being almost incidentally the most delicate *mondaine*. At half past one she takes her *déjeuner*, and at four she begins receiving visitors. Invariably there is a throng of guests, for she admits anyone who is pressed by hardship, listening patiently to all who have cause to complain, always ready with advice, a job for one, hope for another. From between half past five or six until nine or ten she writes, and then she heads to the theatre, goes visiting, strolls the boulevards, or summons order from the abundance of notes, pages and documents at home. She never sleeps before five in the morning.

There are many pictures of her. Marie Coutant, Renoir, and Louise Abbéma have painted her, and at the last Salon Miss Beaury-Saurel captured her fine, capricious little head framed in red curls[169]. The strange, flabby grace, the soft, casual posture, like a water-lily rocked by the waves, the Assyrian gravity of the pale solemn face – before one got closer one might have taken her to be the great Sarah. One was struck by the tragic bearing of her proud appearance, as she sat there in her soft white dress, a tired carnation in her girdle, her long, slender hand hanging down dreamily, and one felt the noble consecration of her stern, just soul. But it lacked that mild, balmy air of warmth and goodness, the powder and splendour and scent of love that attends every one of her gestures. It lacked what François Coppée sang of her: '… *une femme au grand cœur, la bonne Séverine.*'[170] It lacked the delightful, sweet smile around her soft lips, the smile of a child who, presently bathed in tears, receives consolation for her pains.

Fine and soft she chirrups, and in her tender, caressing voice she retains something of the steam and mist of fiery feelings.

'Antisemitism is the faction for the discontented of all factions. Anyone who is aggrieved becomes an anti-semite. There is the nobility, who begrudge the Jews their money and hate them out of envy, revenge and perhaps also out of style, because it is a pose, because it is chic. There is nothing noble or elegant about it, but ultimately it is comprehensible. The Jews have supplanted the nobility. They perform the function it wishes to perform but no longer can. They have the money they wish to have and have no more. So ... beat them to death! That is probably the case everywhere ...'

'It is the same for us.'

'Then the socialists, who are certainly not antisemites, but hold with antisemitism because they welcome any revolt, and because at least it strikes at an element of capital that they hate. They endorse those of its actions that benefit them, without following its doctrine. Of course that is not possible, because it is unjust and contrary to reason, because they strike only the rich Jews instead of the rich in general, and because they strike not just the rich Jews, but the poor Jews as well. But it disturbs order, provokes the mob, it becomes an inconvenience for the government, and that tempts the socialists and attracts those merry Parisians of all parties who entertain no other thought than *embêter le gouvernement*[171]. Aristocrats, socialists and those devotees of uproar who like to ruffle order a little – there you have the elements of antisemitism.'

'And the people?'

'The people? The true, real, genuine people? The people who labour, who create? The people do not trust antisemitism because they sense the lax order, the cunning and falsehood of its arguments, but they are blinded by the charm of a few of its leaders. The people are not antisemitic because they are good and just and peaceful, but many are in favour of Drumont because he is brave, passionate, strong and chivalrous, with a haughty disdain for money, and harsh words for distress. He has written a book, *Le secret de Fourmies*[172], which has wonderful, incomparable pages that speak out against exploitation, against despotism – but of course it always comes back to the Jew, who is to blame for everything and will atone for everything, for every wickedness and violent infamy. But the people like his honest courage, the way he heedlessly calls the intrigues and crimes of the governments by their proper names, which is what the people like about anti-semitism in general, that it unflinchingly voices evil truths that they have long felt but never heard uttered before.'

'Do you believe that antisemitism has a future in your country?'

'Who wants to predict the future? Events always occur in a way that the finest adept could never conceive, and they scoff at every reckoning. The unexpected arises and everything changes. Events occur that no one had suspected, and it is the spirit of events that makes history, not the spirit of the people. Who would want to prophesy? But I believe in a major change in everything, in a mighty revolution. What will happen, how it will happen, nobody knows. I only know, whatever it is, that things cannot get any worse than they are today. Antisemitism may also serve as yeast for fermentation. This may perhaps give it a certain significance in the future, but it will always remain an ugly, crude, disgraceful remedy that offends any just mind. All its arguments are wrong and dishonest. It calls itself Christian? But the Saviour, who was humility and peace incarnate, preached the love of all people and His blood flowed to extinguish all discord from the world, and He left us with His fraternal word that all are equal before God. It calls itself nationalist? Did we applaud the freedom and equality of the Negroes only to now rage against our own citizens? It calls itself social? So all the Jews are rich and the rich never Christian? I know enough Catholic usurers and poor Jews in distress and misery. And if we blame the Jewish spirit for seeking profit, should we not rather blame ourselves for creating it? For centuries we kept them in the ghetto, in shame and contempt. We would not allow them to serve as warriors, or judges, or citizens. They had no fatherland, since they did not defend it, had no king, since they could not approach him, no laws, as they could find no protection in them. What were they to do? They had nothing but trade, usury, the hated professions that others spurned. And now we wish to blame them for that, rather than complaining about ourselves, about the cruel conceit of our ancestors! ... Ah, one could talk for hours against antisemitism, against the poisonous mendacity of its teachings, and against the brutal, raw passion of its form, which arouses the lowest instincts.'

CHARLES MORICE

Charles Morice is something like the Aristotle of the art of tomorrow. He was referred to as the 'mind of Symbolism' because his book on the *Littérature de tout à l'heure*[173], published by Perrin in 1889, sought to clarify the dark wilderness of those fantastical alien verses, to record their objectives and their laws. The book did well. Some mocked its heavy, solemn, diligently pedantic language, and its severe arrogance offended the usual great names, but one sensed a strong mind of rigorous education, prophetic plans and noble desires. Some words have stuck, like the classic formula describing new artists who wish 'to suggest the whole person through the whole art'.

The bourgeois, the good citizen, the dear reader of the old novels in which splendid princes court chaste seamstresses, lamented that the 'young ones' were foreign. They detected German, English traces that are contrary to custom. They found them dark and confused, where the Frenchman loves bright order. They reviled their language, which may well be dreamy and beautiful, but is certainly not French. And their priestly, prophetic, Brahmanic airs made one quake. So it was that over time an entire legend built up around them, as though all the wizards and necromancers were from over there, that land of heavy fog, the black forests of mystical conjurers.

Morice only serves to confirm the legend. He elects to assiduously maintain the pose that the bourgeoisie expect of him from the newspapers. He has, as he trembles about, tall, lean, thin in his wide, loose, dark *robe de chambre*, with his dry, sharp, prickly gestures, with his abrupt, hard nose, with his pale, vapid, earthen countenance with the smudge of a stubborn, short, frizzy beard – he has something gloomy, fantastic, demonic about him, refuted only by his kind, calm, gently ironic eye. A Faust who at the same time has a little Mephisto about him. Or one of those Kreislerian ghosts of E. T. A. Hoffmann[174]. Or a Maurice Barrès, taken from his English habit and dressed in the Devil's livery.

He now gives lectures. In Geneva he spoke about 'the word poetry' and about the 'social principle of beauty' – it was then published by Vanier as *Du sens religieux de la poésie*[175]. And he has just started a series on the 'major questions of the age'. The first one, which he gave two days after my visit, is about antisemitism. He gives me the essence, the most relevant phrases and thoughts.

'I speak as a poet, as an artist. I asked myself: what position does the poet, the thinker, have in today's modern state? And I have found that a society led by lawyers, rather than philosophers, resembles a man who walks on his head and thinks with his feet. What is to blame? What is preventing the natural order of things?

Money. Thus I proceeded from the attitude of the poets and thinkers to questions of money and from money to the Jews, and from the Jews to the antisemites, whom I found foolish, unjust and contrary to culture. What are their complaints? I would rather not say anything about the religious element for it really is far too ridiculous; but the nationalist question no longer suffices, because when a country grants him civil rights, the Jew is the best and most faithful patriot – in 1871, around sixty percent of the Alsatian Jews voted in favour of France. So only the economic concerns remain. But the number of rich Jews is small, and if you were to drive them out, you would not have expelled capitalism; only the Protestant and Catholic opportunists would benefit. So all the teachings of the antisemites are vain, empty and void. They are a denial of the greatest achievement of our past, that great phrase of the revolution that holds the rights of all people to be equal. It is they who actually turn the Jew into that for which they reproach him; they alienate him from the people by persecuting him – and so the Russian Jew is a Jew, the French Jew is French. They damage the culture that requires the Jews – because they bring to this race great, rare, indispensable gifts: their wonderful strength which they have retained through tribulation and persecution, their incomparable minds and ideals of unyielding justice, which must form a complement to the Aryan ideal of love. These are the results of my research.'

GUSTAVE PAUL CLUSERET

General Cluseret is an alien oddity among the people of today. Adventurous rebels of his ilk, with their tremendous appetite for the new, the bright, the exuberant, with their inexhaustible desire to sketch out a great life in heroic strokes – you don't find them anywhere else today. In this time of subtle, rare, carefully curated sensations, he is the last remnant of a wild, impetuous, rapturous drama, the last of the 1830[176] mould with their red vests, crimson passions and scarlet notions.

He was born in Paris on 13 June 1823. His father, a colonel of the infantry, sent him to the school of Saint-Cyr, from which he graduated as a lieutenant. In 1848 he commanded the 22nd Battalion against the barricades and was decorated with the Legion of Honour for his courage. After the coup of Napoleon III, he joined the Council of War in Blidah[177] as imperial commissary. But he soon gave that up to follow Garibaldi, who appointed him lieutenant colonel after the conquest of Capua[178]. When the guns fell silent, he set off across the sea to fight in the American Civil War as adjutant to McClellan; in the corps in which the Comte de Paris and the Duke of Chartres served as mere captains he soon rose to the rank of general[179]. He then founded a newspaper in New York to help elect General Frémont to the presidency[180]. But oratorical disputes could not detain him for long, and he returned from America after the election of General Grant to join the Fenian Revolution[181]. The English courts condemned him to death because he had directed the raid on Chester Castle under the name of Aulif[182], and he fled to France, where he wrote studies on 'the situation in the United States' for the *Courrier français*, but in *L'Art*, a new journal he had founded, he gave such passionate voice to his revolutionary desires that he was sentenced to Saint-Pélagie[183], where he encountered the leaders of the 'Internationale' and learned the concepts of socialism. He left France and only returned after the fall of the emperor in the revolution of 4 September[184]; he spoke out against the Government of National Defence in the *Marseillaise* with such fury, and the pressure of ensuing public outrage was so great that Rochefort, who owned the journal, was forced to disavow him. He fought in the Lyon Revolution of 28 September and established the Commune of Marseille, which elected him Marshal of Southern France[185]. On 16 April 1871 he was appointed to the Paris Commune and then the Executive Committee, but was dismissed on 1 May for his mocking, insolent courage in the face of the revolutionary government, arrested and taken to Mazas[186], from which he only managed to escape in the horrendous turmoil of 24 May when German troops marched on the city[187]. A priest hid him for five months. In November, he succeeded in fleeing to England and then to America. The third council of Versailles[188] had meanwhile sentenced him to death. In 1882, two years after the amnesty, he ventured back to France to head the editorial board of the *Commune*. But the wild, immoderate, raving style in which he wrote immediately brought another complaint – that he was inciting the army to treason, and faced with a prison sentence of two years he had to leave his homeland once more. He was permitted to return in 1884 and with the aim of living apolitically he devoted himself solely to painting, which he had always loved as an amateur; he held an exhibition of 120 of his paintings and sketches, and now you can see his entries in the Salon every year, landscapes and architectural studies from the South and the Orient, in bold, proud, strong colours, but lacking personal merit that might break the mould. In 1888 he was elected to the Chamber for Var against the radical candidate Foroux, the Mayor of Toulon, in 1889 in the second district of Toulon, but his straightforward, awkward passion barely stands out amid the disingenuous dealings of clever rascals and mischievous ruses …

He lives on wide, empty, grey boulevard Arago. The trees are dusty; there are few people about, all is aglow with the sad, wretched air of labour. The round, pale graceful dome of the Val-de-Grâce, the pale monastery Anne of Austria once gave to the Benedictines, beckons darkly.

There are a few houses, three or four, with nothing but painters. The young and the mad, those who still have riots to run, live up there on the noisy, bright slopes of Montmartre, which Salis[189], the master of the Chat Noir, has called the navel of the earth. The famous and pampered, the elect of fashion, have their lavish, bright, invariably uncomfortable and theatrical studios behind parc Monceau, boulevard Malesherbes, avenue de Villiers, rue Prony, in those dainty lodgings for wealthy guests. But those who wish for quiet labour, solitary study or to hearken to themselves, or even those who have turned art into a patient, bourgeois industry, prefer to live in this placid, modest, commercial quartier untroubled by the noise of the mad city. This is where the dreamy Ambros[190] works, he of the gloomy, wild, pale 'child murderers'; now he is assiduously seeking the formula of today's other East and the scruffy, besmirched splendour he experienced there. This is where Marius Michel[191] works, the thoughtful seeker who strives for simple, meagre, chaste expression for rare and special things. It is where our Rudolf Weiß, a brave manufacturer of oriental scenes, works, every month punctually delivering a new group of trading Arabs, or in fact always the same one, only now with the lecherous Moor on the right, the mischievous Jew on the left, and next time they will be reversed, along with clean, smart, fine ornamentation copied from the beautiful, large, clear models of splendid books.

Here one apartment resembles the next. At the front is the large, high, bright hall, with pictures, sketches, easels, fabrics, cushions, weapons, jugs, dolls and costumes; facing the courtyard, which fancies itself a garden, a narrow salon brightened by all manner of colourful novelties; and above, a bleak square for the night-time. One is much like the next, except that Cluseret's has a desk, and the painter's colourful domesticity is strewn with books, papers and files.

He is rough, awkward, clumsy, with a hint of Gabillon[192] in his large, broad, powerful gestures, in the bony voice that casts forth words like blocks. He slips out of his greasy, grey, old smock with wild, gruff conviviality. In his sunken, desolate face, beneath short bristles of white hair, under his damp, empty, cloudy, blinking eyes, his fat, fleshy, blue nose shines like some fantastic cucumber …

'I am a free thinker, an absolute free thinker, a radical free thinker. So for me there is no religious antisemitism, only social. That at least I do not rule out. You would have to be blind. Panama and all the big scams – who is always the first in line? Jews, nothing but Jews. There are Jews I know whom I value and admire immensely. But that does not dispel the fact that all these disgusting scandals of recent years have found their origins and their most resourceful leaders in the Jews. It is to Drumont's credit that he was the first to prove it. It seems irrefutable to me. I have been observing the world long enough now. I am 71 years old, and I have to say, if I think back and compare it to fifty years ago, there was no trace of the horrendous corruption that is rife today, it is solely the fault of the Jews from Germany who threw themselves on our poor country and ruined it.'

'I would have expected you, as a socialist, to blame the entire bourgeoisie.'

'Of course the bourgeoisie, but the Jew is the

clearest and most convenient expression of that, and the Jews are the best teachers of bourgeois crime. Naturally when I refer to Jews I do not mean the poor man who works and starves, and I do not mean just the Israelites, but it is shorthand for all exploiters and swindlers in general. The Jewishness lies neither in the race nor the religion, but in the social position. Without Jews, the bourgeoisie would never have become so mean and dangerous. That is the doing of the Jews and the Protestants – with the Protestants it is exactly the same thing, and a history of corruption in France would be a history of Jewish and Protestant power. These two classes of foreigners share control over us, and it is Germany and England who reap the profits – bear in mind that all our foreign ministers, and most of our ministers of the navy, those incompetent fools, have been Protestants. We must finally rise up against this perpetual betrayal and treason against the people and the state, and the persistence of this state of affairs, symbolised by the Jew, is intolerable. That is why I am an antisemite.'

'But what do you think is the solution to anti-semitism? What means do you suggest?'

He grimaces for a moment and scratches behind his big, thick, bulging ears. Then, gruffly shaking his shoulders – 'The only solution is a thorough change in public spirit. The spirit must be purified and provoked to indignation against the reign of fraud. We need a cleansing and rebirth of morals, in which all the vices of exploitation, which I shall call Jewish for brevity's sake, would no longer be possible.'

'You would not consider an expulsion of the Jews?'

'That is nonsense. First, it does not work, and second, it would be a vile injustice. We do not wish to curtail the rights of the Jews, we just do not want them to curtail ours. We do not wish to suppress them. We just do not want them to rule.'

'Could you contemplate laws against the Jews?'

'Under no circumstances. I would find that completely inadmissible. Such aspirations will find no favour with us. They are far too contrary to the spirit and traditions of our people. I myself would be their first opponent, for they would violate the freedom and equality for which we fight. No, no laws, no violence against the Jews! Let us cast fraud from public life and Jewishness will disappear by itself. An honest disposition is the only remedy against the Jewish model. For me the only meaning in the entirety of antisemitism is that it should arouse such a disposition. That is why it presents cases that enrage and foment, it incites. Especially the horrible accounts from Algiers, where the Arabs, a race of unutterable chivalry and nobility, are indeed horribly enslaved and bled dry by the Jews. This must in time lead the people to reflect upon our own disgraceful conditions. Otherwise there will be no solution to the question. We need a rebirth of morality among the people, which must arise from their own efforts – laws, regulations cannot help. This seems to me the meaning of the antisemitic movement, which – I repeat – is not opposed to a religion, not opposed to a race, but is opposed instead to social ills. I repeat: I have good, old friends who are Israelites without being Jews, and I know a lot of Christians who are very bad Jews. A Jew is merely someone who lives from deception rather than labour. It is only these people that the movement opposes.'

At the door he enquires about Austria, about the young Czechs in particular to whom he is well disposed, and tells of his old comrades, of Bem, Klapka, Kossuth and Pulszky[193]. 'Yes – I have been familiar with just about every struggle for freedom anywhere on earth. I fought for revolution across the whole globe for a while. Later, of course, I found other diversions.'

ALEJANDRO SAWA

When I went to Spain in 1889, word of young Sawa's accomplishments was just beginning to spread through the cities. The innovators rejoiced and even the guardians of the old formulae, alarmed though they were by his impetuous, delirious passion, could not fail to recognise a strong, fertile mind. He seemed irresistible. He seemed highly modern and yet wholly Spanish – modern in his fine sensitivity for the latest problems, yet Spanish in his frenetic desire for the monstrous, for rampaging gigantic figures, for furious forms that have outgrown all humanity, just as Goya and Ribera once raged. *Nadie hay allí que sea normal,* said París, the critical herald of the *Gente Nueva,* when writing about the *Crimen legal,* his boldest, freest creation; there is nothing normal here. It was the ultimate formula of his entire nature, one that could be appended to all of his works.

There are men who are born kings, and, poor though they may be, they never lose the noble gesture, the proud strain, the solemn grace of mastery. That is how he was then – a savage, barbarian king under his helmet of dark locks; in his avid gaze were the embers of Granada, where swarthy *gitanos* languish in gardens of perpetual bloom; his brown cheeks bore the kiss of the Andalusian sun; every gesture Dionysian; a troubadour dreamt by Victor Hugo, a gypsy dreamt by Byron. To see him was to love him, like a wondrous apparition.

He flung four abrupt, defiant works at the world: *La mujer de todo el mundo* (The Wife of All the World), that *Crimen legal*, the *Declaración de un vencido* (The Declaration of a Defeated One) and *La noche* (The Night). Then all at once he fell silent, disappeared, and he was said to be leaving for Paris – vast, endless, alluring Paris. It is here that I have found him once more, deep in the furthest corner of the Latin Quarter, and I recognise the torment of his life, which will either impel a great work, a great deed from his tortured soul, or destroy it.

He had to leave his homeland. He could not stay. He is incapable of dreaming insouciant dreams of real life. The beauty that he feels he wishes to insert into life. He wishes to edify, to convert, to create a free people of noble desire, guided by love. So as an artist who demands art from the world, beauty from life, he wages insurrection against any order that disturbs his dreams. But he could not squander himself in the foolish revolt of his country, in the eternal debates of the secret conventions, where the queen is overthrown nightly, followed by a call to revolution – all those tragic operettas. He had to leave, because hatred prevented him creating at home. But beyond his home it is love that prevents him from creating, because he cannot rid himself of the anxious longing for his land, for the full Spanish sun.

He wanders through Paris, sometimes in fine society with the Marquesa de Alta Villa[194], the blond, gentle, intimate friend of Queen Isabella, with the beautiful Rachilde[195], the bizarre artist of perversion, with Zola, with Zorrilla, before going wild in the student taverns again with Paul Mounet, the great tragedian who is so much like our Martinelli[196], with the lean, satanic Charles Morice, with Paul Verlaine, the drunk, faun-like Socrates, who is now the purest poet, or even weeks, terrible, gloomy weeks alone, *en ours,* cowering in desolate corners, at war with himself, contemptuously disdaining the youthful devotees of Parisian poetry, for they seek only sweet, vain games with rare words, alien rhymes, broad rhythms, instead of dwelling upon the suffering of people and guiding them to happiness. He lives an unstable life and he yearns; he would like to go home and yet he dares not, he wavers and torments himself with a thousand doubts until the time when he is summoned by a great fate, a great hour. He still believes it to be far off and refuses the request of his friends that he should lead the Spanish socialists.

He has become quite Parisian. The wild impetuous curls are thinner, and he is dressed for the boulevard. But there is still a subtle Andalusian flavour to his serene, light elegance that favours colourful, glaring ties and the loudest fabrics.

I tell him of my interview about antisemitism and ask for his opinion.

'Since when you have been in politics? Well, this is new!'

'I am not in politics – and I never will be. You need not fear my competition. But I am an inquisitive spectator at all European comedies – why should I miss the comedy of politics? I do not wish to edify anyone, or convert them. I merely wish to recognise the people of my time, as they think and feel – perhaps only to discover myself all the more clearly, the special and unique in myself amid the contradictions. And also it is highly amusing; some collect beetles, I wish to gather sentiments. So please, would you be so good as to hand over your beetle.'

'There is no arguing with you when you want something. For the love of God!'

'So, let us begin! Do you even have antisemites in Spain? Are you antisemitic? What do you think about the Jews?'

'There is no antisemitism – in any of the parties. Even the worst reactionaries, who otherwise seize any means possible, would be too ashamed. Once in our history we had a fundamental antisemitism – and that shame is indelible. We have been warned. For us, the Jew and the Christian are treated the same. The Castilian is much more foreign to the Andalusian than the Jew is to the Christian. We cannot even tell who is Jewish. The Jews are physically, morally and in their essence completely equal to other Spaniards. The few international Jews who are known as such, like Rothschild and his Spanish agent Bauer[197], do not arouse hatred. We hate money – but you could never persuade a Spaniard that Catholic money is purer, more honest than Jewish money. In short, we are not equipped to answer the question – there is no antisemitism in Spain.'

'And you? As a demi-Parisian, you must be familiar with it.'

'I find it absurd, unjust and mean. I know a lot of Jews here, but I have never felt aversion to any of them. On the contrary – I admire and revere the Jews. I admire the grave, sacred greatness of their art – what may compare to their poetry? I revere their brave spirit, which rejects ancestral lies – who has ever striven so bravely for freedom? A people that can boast Heine, Marx, Lassalle merits glory and love, and it is precisely the Germans, glorified by the shimmer of those names, who owe them eternal thanks. And among them I have found the most splendid people, the finest examples of pure goodness. Look – I will tell you a story about something that happened this winter. I have two friends. One is a Christian, the other a Jew. The Christian is a poet without a sou to his name. The Jew is a banker and is in business. The Jew helps the poet where he can, and they are very close. The Jew has a lover – and he adores her beautiful, funny, delectable mug. He buys the girl a small townhouse, keeps her horses and cares for her with all tenderness. The poet falls in love with her. They cuckold the Jew. Of course they get caught. What happens? What does the Jew do? Anyone else would have shown the friend and the girl the door. The Jew asks the friend: Do you love her? He asks the girl: Do you love him? And as they do not deny it, he says: Then of course you must live together. Only in public should she remain my lover because you have no money to take care of her. And I would like to continue being a friend to both of you. Is that not wonderful? Is that not an unparalleled example of heroic mastery over one's self? And that is why I am revolted by the miserable lies of the antisemites, and their dealings strike me as wretchedly dishonourable, because they merely inhibit, imperil, delay a solution to unavoidable social issues. And now come, let us talk of rational things, of women and verse.'

MANUEL RUIZ ZORRILLA

It was after Serrano's victory on the Guadalquivir in September 1868, when the insurgent generals under Prim drove Isabella[198] out and proclaimed the republic, that he became minister for the first time, at thirty-four years of age. A splendid lawyer, famed in the chamber for the vehement courage of his speeches and now, since the Madrid insurrection of June 1866[199] he retains the glory of exile and the favour of the street. But soon, amid the unheeded doubts of his friends, he too fell into rebuke and disrepute by favouring the young Prince of Genoa[200] over the young Alfonso, the Duke of Montpensier, Dom Fernando of Portugal, King Luís and the Republic, and was forced to resign after a few months. He was elected president of the Cortes and led the radicals, who wavered between the Liberals and the Republicans without any real will of their own. Amadeo[201], to whom he offered the crown in Florence on 4 December 1870, summoned him to the first administration, and after the fall of Serrano he ran operations until 3 October 1871. In the new elections he became a deputy of Madrid, and in June 1872, at the insistence of the monarch, he again formed a cabinet. At that time, when the country was witnessing increased uprisings of Republicans, Internationalists, Carlists and Alfonsists, he swore in his most famous speech to defend the dynasty to the death, to fall in battle for it at the gates of the fortress, and only when the king's courage deserted him and he voluntarily abdicated did he retire to Portugal. He was banished after the coup by Cánovas and Martínez Campos[202] and, not having taken advantage of the 1881 amnesty, lives in quiet solitude in Paris, while incessantly using manifestos to air his demands for a constituent assembly, religious freedom and social reforms.

He lives on the edge of the Bois de Boulogne, on the avenue de la Grande Armée, where the most beautiful street in the world runs from the white place de la Concorde through the Champs-Élysées gardens.

A simple room of no style. No decoration other than numerous pictures of conspirators, orators, writers. Also pictures of Victor Hugo, which bear dedications in his firm, mighty, imperial hand.

He is strong and square, with the neck of a torero. You might take him for an angry, asthmatic, congested major who feels he has been unfairly pensioned off. He does not seem intellectual, but his hard, immobile, iron features, his narrow, sharp, rigid gawking eyes, and the power of his precipitous, heavy chin speak of defiance and grandeur.

I present a letter of recommendation from Sawa and share my request.

'I should very much like to share my opinion on antisemitism. For actual political questions, I would have to refuse. And I do not make a habit of interviews. I was always able to evade the attempts of your French counterparts. You owe it to Sawa, whom I love heartily for his great and courageous talent, that I am making an exception. For with me there is nothing to interview. I do not hide my opinions. They are in my manifestos. And because for many years now I have been used to thinking publicly, further questions are rendered superfluous.'

'But you have never talked about antisemitism.'

'Because it does not exist in Spain! There is no antisemitism because there are no Jews – unfortunately! The expulsion of the Jews was the greatest sacrilege in our country, an unpardonable crime against the future of our people. When we expelled the Moors we expelled culture, with the Jews went industry, trade, all the means of bourgeois prosperity. It is this suicidal rage that caused the unutterable misery of our people. Only a few remained at the time, and this weak, small remnant was absorbed completely into the rest of the population. So we do not have any of the conditions for antisemitism which, by the way, I must confess in all honesty I never understood. That anyone can still be enthusiastically religious today and hate because of religious compulsion, that is a mystery to me. It seems to me such a denial of all culture, of all reason, of all rights, of the modern spirit in general, and of our whole era, that I can find no word of indignation strong enough. It is an unexampled infamy that will leave an indelible mark on our race. That today it is even possible to be antisemitic without shame, and that at a stroke they can eradicate all the work of the past and all the achievements of the spirit – you have to despair of humanity. I find it absurd to even seek reasons against antisemitism. It judges itself. Anyone capable of following its rabble-rousing must be ill, mentally degenerate, and has forfeited any right to a hearing on serious questions.'

HENRI ROCHEFORT

Rochefort recently ruffled Zola a little and Zola, who may be a great artist but is undoubtedly a small man, cannot bear it. There was controversy, stirred up by the press, and so for a week Paris returned to its examination of a question that had exercised it for almost thirty years: whether the man from the *Lanterne*[203] is merely a political clown, in the recesses of history, or an honest, effective force for development of the country. Many spoke up, but none managed to solve it.

Zola said: 'I know him as an amusing man, an incomparable associate, an irresistible conversationalist; but what has always astonished me about him is his gaze – his naive, inane, empty eye. His head seems to me like an empty bell that lacks a clapper. Of course there is no doubt that he has talent. He is someone. He stands out among his peers. But let us examine his life, his work of twenty years, the works that lie in his past! What has he created? Nothing but Boulanger, who was certainly not the salvation of the fatherland. What will remain of him? Nothing but his school of *gobeurs* like Millevoye and Ducret[204] who, after every slander, search for any ridiculous piece of paper stolen by some cheat to create a new scandal with each new day, at any cost!'

Daudet said: 'I do not understand Zola. Rochefort is the finest thinker I know of today. He thinks his eye empty? I find it deep, and at the first glance it reveals a powerful, unusual nature. He has a tremendous talent, an inexhaustible talent, constantly renewed in eternal youth. I read him daily and his strength, his wit, his passion never fail, never weary. Why else would all the deputies in the Chamber and the senators in the Senate read him every morning? They read him because with his rich knowledge of people and things, with his great experience he always arrives at the truth. No one knows every class of society like he does, every station of life. He has lived on the boulevard, he has lived among the nobility, he has lived with artists, he has written comedies, he has written novels, quite fabulous, incomparable novels, he was in prison, he did hard labour, he was in New Caledonia[205] – and now he is banished once more! And what grace he has to say grave things with Gallic cheer – what courage, one that yields not to danger, to distress, to menace!'

Lemaître has written about him before, in his questionable, dubious, forbearing manner which prefers to seek rather than find. He calls him one of the *cas moral des plus intéressants et des plus irritants à la fois, par l'impossibilité où l'on est d'y voir clair jusque au fond*[206], and draws him into all sorts of comparisons, examples and categories, none of which sits quite right. A master of that ceaseless irony, passion and selection known as *blague*, a vaudevillist, an irreconcilable enemy of authority and order who summons the wildest instincts from the street, an apostle of distress who is a king of the boulevard, a revolutionary who cannot forget the Marquis, like one of those predatory knights and ennobled bandits who once railed at all power out of rage, out of conceit, out of warlike lust – these are the kind of words you will find attached to him. Nothing completely describes his bizarre mockery and thus contradictions remain. Perhaps one could solve them in another way. One should not forget that he is an artist – not in marble, paint or words of course, but in living people. Maurice Barrès, who admires and loves him, once praised him for being an incomparable *manieur d'hommes,* and he himself once threatened: *'Je ferai descendre des faubourgs, quand je voudrai, deux cent mille hommes.'*[207] So perhaps one should explain him through this artistry of life which forms its dreams, its vision of the world in humans rather than sound or painting, what they would probably call an *Übermensch* now, if that strange word has any meaning at all.

He lives in Regent's Park and the deep open green of the English countryside murmurs in the delicate, fine Rococo of the sumptuous salon. Outside there is chirping in the broad full trees. But here nimble shimmers scurry from figurines, busts and vases, like marquises smiling at the dance.

Van Beers[208] once painted his pale, sardonic, burlesque skull, which lent the impudent jag of his steep white head above his abrupt forehead something

ANTISEMITISM

fantastically ridiculous, an uncanny jest, like a caricature of Don Quixote. His eye is strange; avid, harking, spying, like a sponge that sucks in, draws in, leaves nothing, like a leech, like a vampire. One feels that one cannot lure – or hide – anything from it.

He has a strange way of speaking; off onto the next thought, which he seizes vigorously and folds into large phrases, with other whims wedged between them, which he immediately drops again, only to return to them straight away. And so his speech turns in circles. It lacks the bright, easy, assured order of his writing.

'Above all: I am a passionate, fanatical antisemite. But I reject all religious antisemitism. It is dumb and stupid. I am an atheist. Faith does not interest me. Religion does not work on me – it has been that way with me since childhood. It is due to my upbringing, since there was no faith in my entire family – my father was a strict Voltairean. This issue has nothing to do with religion either. You need not be a Christian to oppose the Jews. I was in prison in 1871 with Muslims who had a ferocious hatred of the Jews. The only reason that whole uprising of the Arabs took place back then was because Crémieux[209] naturalised the Jews – since that decree the decline of Algiers has been inexorable; it is getting worse with every passing day. Therefore I do not enquire about religion, there is no religion in my family – I was baptised at the age of eleven and a half so I could attend school – but my daughter and my granddaughter were not. But I am antisemitic because I see how the Jews are. The Jews are to blame for all the great catastrophes of my people. And that has always been the case in every country, and every nation has been forced to defend and protect itself against the Jews. The Spanish Inquisition, for instance – most people are not aware that it was originally established to investigate the source of Jewish riches. There are a hundred proofs that the Jew has always been considered a dubious and dangerous creature. The Jews are venal, the Jews are corrupt, the Jews are usurers. In their blood they have a principle that drives them and urges them to seize everything for themselves. In distress they grovel. In power they are implacable. That is why I am an antisemite. The religious reasons I find silly. I detest Catholicism. But look at Panama, the copper story[210] all the major scandals – Jews everywhere! They get in everywhere, they survive everywhere. Napoleon made plenty of kings, all of them disappeared – only the Jewish Bernadottes[211] remained on the throne. They have an incredible talent for getting rich overnight – Baron Spitzer[212], with the famous collection which has now been auctioned and estimated at fifteen million, started out as a very poor devil. And they escape from the most difficult perils – Mr Cornelius Herz, who has given Clemenceau alone over three million, now sits happily in Bournemouth, healthier than you and I together, and knows that nothing will happen to him. See, it is these things that cause antisemitism! That is why in every country and in every era there have always been revolts against the Jews. That is the basis of the whole question.'

'But what kind of solution do you imagine?'

'It goes without saying that I do not want specials laws against the Jews. That would be contrary to all the requirements of the modern spirit. The principle of the same right for all must not be diminished. I do not call for special laws to be applied to the Jews; I merely call for the laws that apply to others to be applied with equal rigour to the Jews – not just when it suits Rothschild, who determines everything these days, according to his whims. I do not oppose equal rights for Jews, I favour equal rights for others. And one ought to punish a Jew if he happens to be a swindler. That is the only way to break their dominance – their dominance over all enterprise, over the press, over society. See Lesseps[213], for instance – I know Lesseps very well; in the whole Panama episode it is the Jews alone who are guilty, with their insatiable greed for profit from every business. Suez would be impossible today, too, because the avarice of the Jews consumes every undertaking. And just look at the press – there is no French press any more, it is all in the hands of the Jews. This, and not for foolish religious reasons which I reject, is why I am an antisemite. I am not interested in reactionary antisemitism that calls for laws against the Jews. I merely oppose the rule of the Jews. Cornelius Herz sat here in this armchair and swore to me that if I followed his propositions, he could end my banishment in two days – the ministers themselves would come in person and ceremonially summon me. Yes, these are conditions that I find intolerable and untenable. Every healthy mind must revolt against them.'

SIR CHARLES DILKE

Charles Wentworth Dilke is the grandson of the great journalist who founded the *Athenaeum* and then the *Daily News* with Dickens, and the son of the zealous entrepreneur who in 1847 created the first exhibition of English industry with Cole and Russell and four years later created the first global exhibition[214]. It was in 1868, when he was twenty-five years old, that he was elected to the seat of Chelsea, distinguishing himself with a knowledge of foreign affairs drawn from long journeys throughout Egypt, India, Australia, California and the United States, and by his republican sentiments, which even after his defeat in the 1874 elections he shared in an impudent, satirically audacious pamphlet on *The Fall of Prince Florestan of Monaco*[215]. In 1880 he joined Gladstone's cabinet and renewed the trade treaty with France. He was brought low by a disgustingly British scandal after he was sued by a cuckold. But he was able to stake his claim in the Liberal party and, through tireless struggle against Salisbury's foreign policies, especially in the Egypt question, soon regained public respect.

He is tall and imposing, with full, broad, healthy features, with ease and cheerful strength in every gesture, with the attributes of a horseman and hunter, a true English squire which he is not at all in spirit, like Prince Starhemberg painted by Pochwalski.

'For me the question does not exist because it does not exist in our country. Here there is no antisemitism, either in society or among the people. At most out in Whitechapel[216], you might sometimes hear statements that sound antisemitic. There is a strong hatred for the Jewish immigrants from Russia. But that has nothing to do with politics. That is nothing but envy, directed not at the Jew but at the rival in business. There is not the slightest trace in society – we have no antisemitism.'

'And do you believe you never will?'

'Never is a big word. Whenever you say "never" in politics it usually happens the next day. But still – I cannot believe it. Antisemitism seems to me impossible in England. We lack all the conditions. We would have to deny our whole history, our culture, all our natural customs. I believe we are safe from its wild agitation.'

'And what do you think about continental antisemitism?'

'To be perfectly honest, one does not concern oneself with it. It seems strange to us and certainly does France and Germany no honour. But we cannot imagine that it will gain in stature in European history. We consider it a disease which will fade of its own accord when its power is exhausted.'

ARTHUR BALFOUR

The nephew of Salisbury. In the House since 1874, Secretary for Scotland in 1886. Notorious for his rigour against the Irish.

To the letter requesting his opinion on antisemitism, he replies[217]:

> Dictated.
> 4, Carlton Gardens, S. W.
> Private. 5th June 1893.
>
> My dear sir,
>
> I beg to acknowledge your letter of the 3rd of June requesting an interview for the purpose of discussing the Jewish question in Europe. I should be glad to give you any assistance in your labours. But in truth there is no Jewish question in England at all and although the problems connected with immigration from Russia and central Europe have excited and still excite a good

deal of attention in this country, this is not because the immigrants are Jews, but because they are paupers. Under these circumstances I fear you would not gain anything from the interview that you desire.

Yours faithfully,
Arthur James Balfour.

HENRY LABOUCHÈRE

Began in diplomatic service in 1854, continued for ten years. In the House since 1864. The leader of radical, republican sentiment, along with Bradlaugh[218]. The most loyal accomplice in Gladstone's Irish policy. There was no doubt that he would be called to his cabinet. But the Queen is implacably opposed to him because in *Truth*[219], which he owns, he often airs truths that are troublesome to the court.

He writes:

'Unfortunately I shall not return to London until the end of the month. Also, I believe I would scarcely be of use to you. I have never dealt with the "Jewish question". I do not allow of it at all, because it is impossible for me to see a question in a difference of religion. So I have no opinion on it.'

ANTISEMITISM

ANNIE BESANT

Annie Besant, brave friend of Bradlaugh who now directs the Buddhist community since Blavatsky's[220] death, once explained in a gentle, sweet and mellow text how she became a Theosophist, first as a devotee, then a fanatical messenger of Materialism. But ultimately the only means she found of solving the compulsion of a thousand doubts, the eternal enigma, was through the sacred law of karma, which holds that every human life is determined by the merits and misdeeds of a past life, and that our merits and misdeeds will in turn determine the life to come. And it was only in silently, devotedly cultivating purification, following the example of the great masters, until the bestial was stilled and secret voices spoke forth from her mind, that her restless spirit finally found reconciliation and peace.

Buddhism, Theosophy – many are startled by these words and think immediately of wild spectres. They would be advised to make their way to the Theosophical Society headquarters on Avenue Road, at the edge of Regent's Park. There are two bright, narrow houses set amid roses and lilacs, beetles humming, butterflies fluttering, the wind bending the branches, a rustling cheerful profusion. You come to a small sitting room where strange bronzes lend a fine, bizarre consecration, pictures of whimsical, pale, ecstatic heads and the colourful delights of Japanese ornamentation. It is enough to make you forget the broad, brown wastelands of English dwellings where one always feels oneself to be aboard the Orient Express.

I am met by Mead, the Secretary-General of the society. Gaunt, slender, quiet, with faint, shy, anxious gestures, softly spoken with just a trace of irony, with a pale, thin bloodless face framed by a sparse, reddish fringe, like a sickly prince painted by Velásquez. He tells me about the programme of the society, which was established in New York on 17 November 1875. It has three objectives: to form a great brotherhood of all peoples, regardless of race, creed, sex, caste or colour; to promote knowledge of Oriental literatures, religions and philosophies; and to study the unknown laws of nature and psychic powers that dwell secretly within us.

'You see, there is not a trace of witchcraft or Satanism. On the contrary – we are always a little sceptical of hysterical disciples who come to us with their frenzied delight in clandestine enchantments – hence the dispute with the French[221]. And there you will at once find the answer to your question: for us there can be no antisemitism. To us, every faith and every race is equal. We seek the eternal beyond perishable forms.'

He leads me to the hall where they conduct their

ceremonies, with its austere symbols from all religions, shows me their writings, books, journals in the large library, where Schmiechen[222] painted the gloomy, heavy, pained head of Blavatsky, and brings me to Besant.

She is short, slender and shy, awkward and subdued in manner, humble in posture and gesture, her expression sad beneath a short, white fringe. Eschewing finery and fashion, she is studiously stark and sober in bearing, like a sketch of an English governess. But her deep, child-like grey eyes light up.

'Naturally we are opposed to antisemitism. Any movement against a race or a faith seems unjust and foolish to us. Incidentally, I do not believe that one can really speak of antisemitism in England. There is none. That which may at times resemble it has nothing to do with the Jews. For some it is hatred of the great forces in the stock market; for others, out in the East End, where they do not care for Russian immigration, it is the fear of cheap labour that spoils prices – much like American agitation against the Chinese. Since these complaints do not pertain to anything exclusively Jewish, we may well boast that our country knows no antisemitism.'

SIDNEY WHITMAN

The friend of Bismarck, who wrote *Imperial Germany* and *The Realm of the Habsburgs*, one of the great mediators between the peoples, Phoenicians of the intellect such as Hillebrand, Georg Brandes and Juan Valera[223], who transgress the frontiers of their own nations to lovingly penetrate others and draw out from them that which is human, that which always bears similarities despite the change of forms.

A quiet room, with that broad, dark comfort of British taste. Engravings by Whistler, paintings by Lenbach[224]; one with the laconic note: 'Failed' – Franz von Lenbach. All manner of mementoes of Bismarck and Moltke[225]. And when he opens his files, all the great names of Europe march forth. He does not travel as others do – to see streets and buildings and things of other countries – but to meet the powerful leaders who decide the fate and spirit of the peoples.

He confirms to me that England knows no antisemitism, and he does not believe that will change.

He recently wrote about continental antisemitism in an English monthly[226]. He repeats the most important parts to me.

'Anyone who wishes to recognise the movement must separate antisemitism from the antisemites. The antisemites are mostly unreliable and unpleasant people. They fib, with all sorts of allegations that they cannot prove in court, and they slander. They lack the ethics of accuracy. Yet many follow them because they instinctively feel that there is something in antisemitism. The Jews should not misjudge this and instead realise that hatred of Judaism can very well dwell alongside a great respect for the individual Jew. In fact they should themselves examine the deficiencies that turn people against them. Perhaps it would then become apparent that they lie not in the Jews, but in modern development. That money is not "earned" these days but "gained", that it is not the creator of a thing who counts but the "maker" who "launches" it or "pushes" it, that fraud prevails over labour – is that exclusively Jewish? The Jew is merely a convenient and conspicuous example. But if the movement is to have a serious impact, then it will have to turn away from the Jews and address all moral dangers and demand an ethical purification of public affairs.'

TIM HEALY

Since the death of Parnell, the member for Longford has led the Irish, and we will probably soon see him installed as Secretary for Ireland.

Short and sharp, a thin brown beard with grey tints, a fine, slender nose with nervous nostrils, tiny, gentle, intelligent eyes beneath a rounded forehead. A heavy, grave, awkward dignity in his gaze, in his gestures, rendered comical by his small figure, like a nimble little lizard that has turned stiff and solemn. Most likely he is aware of this himself, and he seems to delight in it if one may judge from the scampering shimmers in the sharp furrows around his mouth.

'Ireland has no antisemitism and has never had it. For the Irish Catholics it is a point of honour that Jews among them have never been persecuted. Where one may have detected antisemitic traces in recent years, this was merely among the lowest orders, and there were particular reasons for it. The Jews who come from Russia roam the country as pedlars, offer credit to the poor, and of course there are always court cases. In one of them a judge, incensed by the back-and-forth lies of the parties, made the careless and irritating statement: "I no longer believe the Jews at all!" That then became a welcome opportunity for the English to revile us and foment against us. The affair was terribly exaggerated and exploited so that we could be accused of intolerance and religious fanaticism and all manner of vices. But in truth a single word, thoughtless and spoken in anger, does not prove anything about an entire people, and as I said, if one were to find inclinations among us that could be interpreted as antisemitic, then it would only be among the rabble. The middle classes are not affected by this aberration. They are tolerant and just. They have sympathy and respect for the Jews. They admire their incomparable, truly princely philanthropy, giving millions as we may give a penny. Any educated person would be ashamed to speak against their race or their beliefs. That there are those who envy their power, their wealth, their bold undertakings, who would deny that? That one may often permit oneself a jest that may seem a little malicious – but these are just idle pleasantries. There is no serious antisemitism either here or in England, and I hope that will not change in the future.'

PAUL JANSON

The leader of the Belgian radicals, the great orator of republicanism and socialism, the indefatigable defender of universal suffrage – *membre de la Chambre des représentants* – and, of course, a lawyer like any Belgian who wishes to make something of himself.

He is short, broad and nimble. His cheeks, his mouth seem to be displaced, pressed, crushed by his hard, heavy, solid forehead. His abrupt crooked nose, like a beak, and the crest of long, grey strands lend him a disputatious, rabulistic air, much as Meixner played Vanssen[227]. Rapid, busy gestures tell of extensive negotiation, in the manner of Clemenceau. Short, sharp and hurried in speech and gesture.

'There is no antisemitism here. It is true that my colleague Mr Edmond Picard, a fine, meritorious thinker who is always chasing the latest paradoxes, held a lecture on antisemitism which agitated violently against the Jews, and another colleague, Deputy Robert, defended them against his unjust complaints in another lecture.

But it is a dispute in which the public has no interest at all. They understand that one may defend oneself against the excesses of speculation, the excrescence of capitalism and agiotage, but they have no interest in hatred of a race, or a belief. They are astonished that the kind of things the French antisemites get up to are even possible today, and are powerless to explain it. Personally, I am an absolute opponent of any kind of antisemitism. I find it shameful, unjust, outrageous. When one thinks that we can still witness something like the persecution of the Russian Jews in this century – it is a scandal for the entire age. But as I said, our country may boast that it is entirely free of it. Even in the clerical faction you will not find a single symptom of any kind of hostility to the Jews. I am certainly not inclined to sing the praises of the clerics, but they do respect public opinion and submit to mores once they recognise them as unassailable. And for us, freedom of conscience, tolerance of other religions and respect for all creeds are indeed unassailable. So firmly and profoundly is this anchored in the people that there is no party that would dare to essay antisemitism.'

EDMOND PICARD

You often hear his name here, whether in connection with politics or art. It arises again and again. He is the refrain of every conversation. When people say of an opinion or a fashion that it has no place in the country, that it has no followers, they always add, 'Except, of course, Edmond Picard!' They say this with cunning glee, and everyone smirks. And then they remember that a foreigner is in their midst and assure him: 'By the way, he is the most subtle and cleverest thinker we have – but just a little mad.' So one hears that his intellect is revered by all, but nobody takes him seriously; they admire his talent, but suspicion accrues to any matter in which he takes the lead. He is a lawyer, jurist and poet. Renowned for his defence in the T'Kindt and Peltzer trials[228], and beyond his homeland as well, having once addressed the court in Paris where his compatriot Camille Lemonnier was tried as a pornographer for a story in *Gil Blas*[229]. The prime theoretician of Belgian law – in countless pamphlets and in the thirty-nine volumes of *Pandectes belges*[230]. As a poet he is the darling of the 'Jeunes' – one need only hear how gratefully, loyally, enthusiastically Maeterlinck[231] speaks of him. He leads the *Journal des tribunaux* and *L'Art moderne*[232].

'I have been preoccupied by the Jewish question since my journey through Morocco. It was there that I first noticed the difference between the Jewish and European races. I have since researched tirelessly – not like Drumont, who collects anecdotes – rather I sought the principles of the Jewish people throughout their history, the dominant strains in the Semitic soul. I have come to the conclusion that there is great danger in granting liberty to Jews, who have an entirely different psychology, a very different way of thinking and feeling to us, even if they adopt our dress and our customs, and that they exert a ruinous influence with their economic, political and journalistic power. I believe I have proven this in my book on the *Synthèse de l'antisémitisme*[233] and in my lectures. The religious aspect is of no importance. But through their money they have succeeded in attaining mastery over Europe and I intend to defend the autochthonous against this foreign domination. That is the result of my research. But, of course, for the time being I remain alone. Nobody else has the courage of antisemitism because nobody wishes to take on Jewish power. And so there is no antisemitic book, no antisemitic newspaper, no antisemitic party – yes, and no antisemites apart from me. But I do not doubt that ultimately the Jewish economy will exhaust the patience of the people. Only recently we had an event that astonished many – Richard's revelations in the Chamber about Argentine assets in Belgium. Such crimes against the masses will gradually lead people to recognise the Jewish peril, as they have in other countries. That it has taken so long here can be explained by the history of the country, by the long struggle between Catholics and liberals; every criticism of the Jews was seen as a test of religious intolerance; one defended and protected them to prove that one was opposed to Catholicism, a freethinker. These views still prevail. But since the Jewish question has assumed a more social character and there is an ever-growing danger that over time, all public power will be turned over to a foreign race – one may well expect our country to follow the example of others without delay. Then they will finally open their eyes and recognise the workings of the Jews, those parasites who only ever enrich themselves without creating anything. Of course they tell me that they are few in number, that we have none at all in the Chamber and only one in the Senate, Mr Levi, successor to Mr Bischofsheim, who was also a Jew, that the press is by no means Jewish – and so on. They may be small in number but their power is all the greater, and they control all the major businesses with tireless zeal to supplant all Christian enterprises, in which they are increasingly successful. Twenty years ago Count Langrand-Dumonceau coined the slogan of "Christianisation of capital"[234]. He had no luck, and after his fall Mr Bischofsheim said: "You see – to Christianise capital means to plant a cross upon it!" Since then, the financial power of the Jews has only grown and things are getting worse every day. It makes me hope that the people will finally gather courage and that I will soon surrender the honour of being the only antisemite in Belgium.'

CHARLES BULS

The mayor of Brussels is tall, slender, lithe, with the free, elegant posture of a fencer or dancer, flexible and swift. A firm brush of short, white hair; his beard in French lace. His nose is sharp, long and hard; his grey eyes are sidling spies, enquiring without yielding anything in return.

'We have no antisemitism. The same laws, the same rights, the same duties apply to the Jews as to everyone else. Here we cannot even discern who is Jew and who is Christian; we do not even pay attention to religious denomination; and nobody wishes to change that. Mixed marriages are common, and that is the best means of blurring all differences. On occasion some rabble-rousing rag of the extreme clerical faction would try to whip up enthusiasm for foreign antisemitism. But then they would be forced to drop it immediately, because even among the Catholics there was no inclination, no comprehension. In our old aristocracy, which is purely Catholic, Jews of status and significance are treated just like anyone else. Here we look to the person, not the race or faith, and our entire history, our entire upbringing, all the habits, opinions and customs of our people guarantee that it will remain so.'

HENRIK IBSEN

Henrik Ibsen writes to me from Christiania[235]:
'I cannot say anything about antisemitism because I find the whole movement completely incomprehensible and unfathomable.

With very best regards,
Yours faithfully,
Henrik Ibsen.'

BJØRNSTJERNE BJØRNSON

I sent three questions to Bjørnstjerne Bjørnson:

1. Is there any antisemitism in Scandinavia?

2. Or are there at least indications that it may exist in the future?

3. What do you think of our continental antisemitism?

He replies laconically:

1. No.

2. No.

3. Hatred of capitalism has gone astray.

AUTHOR'S CONCLUSION

I promised that I would listen to a few people talking about antisemitism; and so it came to be; the documents that would 'show how the educated among the different peoples, the different nations think today,' have been assembled. Germans, Belgians, British, Irish, French, Spaniards and Scandinavians were questioned. I was able to omit Italy as the *Neue Freie Presse* took on this part of my work with commendable collegiality[236].

I found the issue to be different in each country. German antisemitism is reactionary, a revolt of the petty bourgeoisie against industrial development, of 'Germanic' virtue against the liberty of the modern age. Parisian antisemitism is revolutionary, opposed to the accumulation of money and the rule of the rich, merely using the Jew as a convenient and effective example of the capitalist. In Spain, England and Scandinavia there are no antisemites. In Belgium there is only one. All sorts of reasons were expounded for and against antisemitism. But they seem ineffectual. My suspicion – that it in fact arises from a particular disposition of the nerves, a hysterical desire – was confirmed. Many crave the emotion offered by passion, tempest, intoxication of the soul. Finding no great love in this forlorn era, they sup instead on the narcosis of hate. All we need do is find an ideal for them.

[1] Emil Auspitzer, the co-editor (with his brother Wilhelm) of the Viennese newspaper *Deutsche Zeitung* for which Bahr conducted these interviews

[2] These prefatory remarks were originally printed before Bahr's interview with Friedrich Spielhagen, the first in the series to be published in the *Deutsche Zeitung* on 25 March 1893.

[3] Maurice Barrès (1862–1923) was a French writer whose interests, like Bahr's, encompassed both politics and literature. He was a major figure of French right-wing thinking around the time of the Belle Époque, a noted antisemite and Wagner enthusiast.

[4] Henri Rochefort, French politician interviewed later in the book

[5] Hohenzollernstrasse – since 1990 Hiroshimastrasse – connects the Landwehr Canal with the Tiergarten (park) in what is now Berlin's embassy district.

[6] Spielhagen was the first Chairman of the Litterarische Gesellschaft (Literary Society), formed in Berlin in 1888, of which Bahr was a member; other members included Theodor Fontane, Johannes Schlaf and Arno Holz.

[7] It was from the German left wing, specifically Ferdinand Lassalle, that pejorative use of the term *Manchestertum*, or 'Manchesterism' first appeared, referring to the radical free market principles that underpinned the enormous growth of the world's first industrialised city.

[8] To forestall the demands of socialists, Otto von Bismarck had introduced the world's first comprehensive social welfare measures, with legislation ushering in health cover and accident insurance for workers in 1883 and 1884 respectively; these were followed by further bills introducing pension and disability insurance in 1889.

[9] German-Jewish poet Heinrich Heine (1797–1856), one of the major figures of literary Romanticism

[10] Baruch Spinoza (1632–1677), Dutch philosopher of Portuguese-Jewish extraction

[11] The idealised figure of Viktoria (popularly known as 'Goldelse' for her metallic covering) topped the Siegessäule, or Victory Column, which at the time stood before the Reichstag, later to be moved to the Grosser Stern, a major intersection in the central Berlin park, Tiergarten. The original contains a pun on *Verhältnisse*, a word that means both 'proportions' and 'relationships'.

[12] The same 'long, long street' referred to in the Spielhagen interview; Theodor Barth lived in an apartment building at Tiergartenstrasse 37 that housed other liberal figures such as politician Friedrich Kapp, banker and politician Georg von Siemens and another Bahr interviewee, Heinrich Rickert, as well as the premises of Barth's journal *Die Nation*.

[13] The Freisinnige Partei, a liberal party formed in 1884 which split in 1893, not long after this interview

[14] Barth served as *Syndikus* (secretary, or company lawyer) in the Bremen Chamber of Commerce from 1877 to 1883 and first came to wider attention in that role for his opposition to Bismarck's protectionist policies.

[15] Barth founded the liberal weekly *Die Nation* in 1883 and was its editor until 1907; Bahr had six articles published in the journal in the early 1890s.

[16] Jules Lemaître (1853–1914), French writer and critic

[17] Johannes von Miquel (1828–1901), Prussia's Finance Minister, who introduced tax reforms in the kingdom but failed in his attempt to extend them to the empire

[18] An economic policy that defines silver as a standard of monetary value alongside gold

[19] A form of debt relief introduced in Athens in the 6th century BC which also served to reduce debt-related slavery and serfdom

[20] Anti-regime conspirators in 1st-century Rome

[21] This is the first of a number of references to politician Hermann Ahlwardt (1846–1914), one of the most outspoken advocates of politicised, racial antisemitism in Germany prior to the rise of the Nazis. At the time of writing Ahlwardt was a relatively new member of the Reichstag for the far-right German Reform Party and had recently made a name for himself with allegations of Jewish perfidy in a scandal concerning manufacturing faults in rifles supplied to the German armed forces.

[22] Count Georg Leo von Caprivi, Chancellor of the German Empire at the time of writing, having succeeded Otto von Bismarck in 1890

[23] The contentious *Militärvorlage* (Army Bill) was originally proposed by Caprivi in 1892, and foresaw a stronger army while reducing compulsory service from three to two years. Its failure led to the dissolution of the Reichstag in 1893.

[24] Nationalist, right-wing, antisemitic newspaper associated with Adolf Stoecker, court chaplain to the first Kaiser

[25] Politician Eugen Richter (1838–1906), head of the Free-Minded Party of which Barth was a member at the time, who published a dystopian novel predicting the dire consequences of socialism

[26] A street in the Schöneberg district of Berlin then at the southern edge of the city

[27] Swedish writer Ola Hansson (1860–1925) had recently moved to Berlin, fleeing his homeland's censorious reaction to his Decadent works and their lurid eroticism.

[28] The International Workers' Congresses in July 1889 which launched the Second International; Bebel represented Germany along with Wilhelm Liebknecht.

[29] In 1889, left-wing Austrian politician Ferdinand Kronawetter was quoted in the Viennese newspaper *Neue Freie Presse* as saying that 'Antisemitism is nothing but the socialism of the fools of Vienna'. After Bebel paraphrased the axiom in his talk with Bahr, it was often erroneously attributed to Bebel himself, and continues to appear under his name to this day. In context we can see that Bebel's own views on the 'Jewish question' are actually more ambivalent than this quote suggests.

[30] The 'Gewehr 88' was a rifle introduced in 1888 and used by armed forces in Germany and elsewhere for decades. Initial models from Loewe & Co. were plagued by manufacturing faults; Ahlwardt concocted the *Judenflinte* ('Jew Guns') scandal in 1892 by claiming that this was the result of deliberate sabotage on the part of the Jewish-owned company working in the interests of France.

[31] Isidor Loewe, the owner of Loewe & Co. at the time, having taken over from his brother Ludwig; Ahlwardt lost a defamation case brought by Loewe and was sentenced to a five-month prison sentence, which was commuted on the grounds of parliamentary immunity.

[32] In March 1893, Ahlwardt made wide-ranging accusations in the Reichstag of a Jewish-backed financial scandal, claiming that Finance Minister Johannes von Miquel was one of the conspirators.

[33] Presumably Ernst Lieber of the Centre Party

[34] An indirect reference to the Panama Scandal in France which broke in 1892, with significant antisemitic elements which was still the subject of heated debate at the time of writing

[35] *Die Reichsglocke* (or *Deutsche Reichsglocke*) was a Catholic journal

which held Jews to be complicit in Bismarck's *Kulturkampf* against Catholic influence; Otto Glagau and Rudolf Meyer were journalists who claimed deliberate Jewish involvement in the economic slump that dominated the early phase of the German Empire.

[36] This refers to a typically convoluted accusation by Ahlwardt concerning corruption in the construction of railways.

[37] This stretch of railway was a key link in getting coal from the Ruhr to Berlin and other points east, and was established by Bethel Henry Strousberg, the Jewish 'Railway King'.

[38] Charlottenburg, site of the Hohenzollern royal palace, was then a separate city, only incorporated into Berlin in 1920; it was connected to central Berlin by a horse-drawn tram. Marchstrasse started at the Landwehr Canal and led through what is now the Technical University of Berlin; having survived a fire in 1880 that claimed priceless documents, Mommsen's house was destroyed in the Second World War.

[39] Adolf Friedrich, Graf (Count) von Schack (1815–1894) was a poet and collector who maintained an outstanding private gallery of German works from the Romantic and Biedermeier eras in his Munich home, on Brienner Strasse, which Bahr had visited and greatly admired in 1890. After Schack's death the collection was bequeathed to Kaiser Wilhelm II but remained in Munich intact, and is now housed in a neo-classical building on Prinzregentenstrasse.

[40] *Fliegende Blätter* (Loose Leaves) was a satirical journal first published in Munich in 1845, continuing for a century and achieving its peak of popularity around the time Bahr was writing; Adolf Oberländer was one of its most renowned caricaturists.

[41] Hermann Ahlwardt was known as the '*Rektor aller Deutschen*' by his faithful followers; the antisemitic agitator had actually been a rector (headmaster) of a primary school in Berlin, but was dismissed in 1889 for embezzling money intended for his pupils' Christmas party.

[42] Mommsen had in fact undertaken something similar, if on a smaller scale, in 1880 following his dispute with Heinrich von Treitschke. The *Notabeln-Erklärung* (Declaration of Notables) was an open letter printed in the *Nationalzeitung* that emphatically rejected the political, racial antisemitism then on the ascendant, particularly in Berlin. Lawyers, academics, public officials and industrialists numbered among the signatories, who included Bahr's interviewees Pastor J. Schmeidler, Heinrich Rickert and Wilhelm Foerster.

[43] Bruno Hildebrand (1812–1878), German economist representing the 'historical' school of economics with which Schmoller was aligned

[44] Eduard Lasker (1829–1884), was a German-Jewish politician, a key figure of the German Liberal movement who brought public attention

to financial scandals in the early German Empire. In an essay entitled 'Hermann Schulze-Delitzsch und Eduard Lasker', originally published in 1884 and anthologised in *Zur Sozial- und Gewerbepolitik der Gegenwart* (On Social and Commercial Law of the Present Day, 1890), Schmoller writes: 'All moderate elements should realise that a strong and one-sided emphasis on Jewish and Christian orthodoxy will exacerbate the ugly aspects of the existing racial conflict. Peaceful and harmonious coexistence of Christians and Jews is conceivable only on the basis of common moral convictions; and these are partly provided by common schooling, common state institutions, common history, etc., but ultimately they rely on Kantian-Schleiermacherian ethics, on those philosophical convictions that provide the keynote for the beliefs of every Christian and Jew pervaded by the true civilization of the nineteenth century. [...] I believe that I am then all the more entitled to oppose those elements of Judaism that are not yet pervaded by German civilization or German nineteenth-century morality; I am thinking in particular of some of our wholesalers, stockbrokers and entrepreneurs, as well as the numerous pawnbrokers, money brokers and usurers who are ruining our peasantry.'

[45] Presumably refers to Victor Hehn's *Zur Charakteristik der Römer* (On the Characteristics of the Romans, 1843)

[46] Johann Gottlieb Fichte: '*Gleich sei alles, was Menschenantlitz trägt*' (everything that bears a human countenance is equal)

[47] In late 1892, Harden published two articles satirising Kaiser Wilhelm II and his followers, 'Monarchen-Erziehung' (Education of Monarchs) and 'König Phaeton' (King Phaeton) and was subsequently tried for lèse-majesté but acquitted, with the judge noting the articles contained 'irrefutable truths'.

[48] *Die Nation*, liberal weekly journal founded by interviewee Theodor Barth

[49] *Die Gegenwart*, journal established by Paul Lindau

[50] Jules Lemaître (1853–1914), Anatole France (1844–1924), Octave Mirbeau (1848–1917), all prominent French critics

[51] Presumably Karl Frenzel (1827–1914), theatre critic

[52] Georg Brandes (1842–1927), prominent Danish critic

[53] Ferdinand Brunetière (1849–1906), French critic

[54] Johann Wolfgang von Goethe's *Italienische Reise* (Italian Journey), published between 1813 and 1817, recalling his travels of around 30 years prior

[55] 'A good critic is one who relates the adventures of his soul amid masterpieces' (from *La vie littéraire*, 1888)

[56] Paul Lindau (1839–1919), noted author, dramatist and founder of *Die Gegenwart*

[57] **Author's footnote:** Collected in two volumes. Verlag von Georg Stilke,

Berlin [Harden began using the pseudonym 'Apostata' for his most cutting satirical articles in 1890]

[58] The huge Hotel Kaiserhof in the government district of central Berlin was the scene of major events such as the Berlin Congress which carved up Africa between colonial powers, as well as day-to-day encounters between politicians, journalists and high society.

[59] Albert Wolff (1835–1891), German-born French critic, Émile Blavet (1828–1924), French writer, librettist and *chroniqueur*, Henry Fouquier (1838–1901), French drama critic

[60] Franz Mehring (1846–1919), German Social Democrat and editor of the *Volks-Zeitung* newspaper, who moved further left in later life

[61] Josef Kainz (1858–1910), Austrian-born stage actor fêted throughout German-speaking Europe

[62] Café Bellevue, an establishment with a terrace attached to the Hotel Bellevue on Potsdamer Platz

[63] Presumably refers to the bankers Anton Wolff of Hirschfeld & Wolff, and the Sommerfeld brothers of Hermann Friedländer & Sommerfeld; Jewish traders, particularly from eastern Europe, were associated with the Leipzig Trade Fair from the 17th century onward.

[64] Shem, Jewish patriarch and source of the term 'Semitic'; Uriel da Acosta (1585–1640) and Baruch Spinoza (1632–1677), both philosophers of Portuguese-Jewish extraction; Ludwig Börne (1786–1837) and Heinrich Heine (1797–1856), German-Jewish writers; Ferdinand Lassalle (1825–1864) and Karl Marx (1818–1883), German-Jewish instigators of left-wing thinking

[65] From a posthumously published letter by the Frankfurt-born Ludwig Börne, written in 1822: 'My aversion to traders, and Jews as such reached its highest point when I was far from Frankfurt and I discovered what it meant to truly enjoy life.'

[66] Paul Eugène Bontoux (1820–1904), French industrialist and banker who headed Union Générale at the time of its collapse, an inspiration for Émile Zola's novel *L'Argent*

[67] The bank Hermann Friedländer & Sommerfeld, which collapsed in 1891

[68] 'For me, Jews are men like any other. If they are apart, it is because they have been put there.' from Émile Zola's 1891 novel, *L'Argent* (Money), a later instalment of his 'Rougon-Macquart' novels

[69] Leo Tolstoy (1828–1910) was a highly influential figure at the time, particularly in Germany, as much for his reformist, utopian ideals as for his major novels.

[70] The esoteric, syncretic Theosophical Society formed by Madame (Helena) Blavatsky won numerous adherents in Germany, and was an influence on Rudolf Steiner and his own Anthroposophical Society.

[71] Ludwig Büchner (1824–1899) and Karl Vogt (1817–1895), German scientists and key proponents of Materialism

[72] Presumably the Deutsche Gesellschaft für ethische Kultur (German Society for Ethical Culture) formed in 1892 by Wilhelm Foerster (another Bahr interviewee) and Georg von Gizycki

[73] Egidy's first and most influential book, 1890

[74] Hermann Settegast (1819–1908) was a German agronomist who in 1892 formed the Grand Lodge of Prussia, known for its large Jewish contingent.

[75] Johannes Lehmann-Hohenberg (1851–1925), German geologist who funded the journal *Einiges Christentum* (United Christianity), established in 1892

[76] The Moabit district of Berlin, then as now home to the city's main Criminal Court as well as penitentiaries

[77] Gotthardt Kuehl (1850–1915), Walter Firle (1859–1929), Dora Hitz (1856–1924), German artists known for their domestic scenes, the latter a friend of Bahr's

[78] Georg von Gizycki (1851–1895) philosopher and co-founder of the German Society for Ethical Culture (the ensuing quotation is from his notes for the society's founding programme), Heinrich Hart (1855–1906) and Wilhelm von Polenz (1861–1903), Naturalist authors

[79] Martin Luther stayed at the Hotel Schwarzer Bär in Jena on multiple occasions in the early 16th century; the square on which it stands is now named for him. In July 1892, former Chancellor Otto von Bismarck stayed at the hotel when he visited Jena, where he was honoured with a torchlight procession. The Iron Chancellor addressed two groups during his stay, the first, smaller one in the Bär which is the source of the quotation, the second, larger gathering on Jena's market square the next day.

[80] The first *Burschenschaft* (a student organisation comparable to a fraternity) was formed in Jena in 1815; it embodied hopes for a united German nation in the wake of Napoleonic rule. It is thought to be the first organisation to use the national colours of Germany still in use to this day – black, red and gold. These were also the colours of Bahr's *Burschenschaft*, Albia.

[81] Wagner, who refers to himself as 'ein Feind von allem Rohen' (enemy of all roughness) and is famulus (student's assistant) to the titular hero of *Faust*, by Johann Wolfgang von Goethe

[82] **Author's footnote:** See the now-famous essay in the March edition of the *Freie Bühne* of 1892. [In 1892, Prussian Education Minister Robert von Zedlitz-Trützschler introduced a proposal aimed at greater religious influence in schooling, a ploy to win support from the largely Catholic Centre Party. Haeckel's article 'Die Weltanschauung des neuen Kurses'

expressed his fierce opposition to the proposal, which ultimately failed.]

[83] *Natürliche Schöpfungsgeschichte* (1868), published in English as *The History of Creation* (1876)

[84] Friedrich Schiller (1759–1805), at the time professor of history and philosophy in Jena, expressed initial enthusiasm for the French Revolution, contrasting it in a letter to his sister-in-law Caroline von Beulwitz with the scholars in the university town and their 'grim faces' that 'frighten off anything that breathes liberty and joy.'

[85] Julius Langbehn's *Der Rembrandtdeutsche* (The Rembrandt German, 1892), was the less successful follow-up to his hugely popular 1890 work *Rembrandt als Erzieher* (Rembrandt as Teacher), its title an allusion to Friedrich Nietzsche's 1874 essay 'Schopenhauer als Erzieher'.

[86] This appears to be a (slightly altered) quotation from François de Salignac de La Mothe-Fénelon: *Jeune, j'étais trop sage/Et voulais tout savoir;/Je n'ai plus en partage/Que badinage* (I was too wise when I was young/And wished to know it all;/Now I have nothing more to share/But banter).

[87] The United States passed the 'Chinese Exclusion Act' in 1882 (renewed in 1892) in response to resentment against cheap Chinese labour in California; around that time, some politicians in the state stoked anti-Chinese sentiment to gain votes.

[88] In the mid-1880s, Bahr studied under Wagner, as well as Gustav Schmoller, while attending university in Berlin.

[89] 'The most dangerous enemy of the truth and freedom amongst us is the compact majority' (Henrik Ibsen, in *An Enemy of the People*)

[90] *Freie Bühne für modernes Leben* (Free Stage for Modern Life), a short-lived literary journal established in 1890 by Berlin publisher Samuel Fischer (who issued the book version of Bahr's *Antisemitism*). As well as submitting a number of articles, Bahr worked for the journal although he left the same year after a dispute with the publisher.

[91] The Panama Scandal in France (see note 34) and its antisemitic component would have been fresh in the minds of readers; Hermann Ahlwardt attempted to foment similar anti-Jewish feeling in Germany with accusations of corruption among industrialists and government figures.

[92] Dr Hertwig, lawyer, who defended Hermann Ahlwardt in the *Judenflinte* ('Jew Guns') trials

[93] A town in Brandenburg, divided by the German-Poland border after the Second World War

[94] A relatively moderate branch of conservatism with a large component of aristocrats

[95] Karl von Huene of the Centre Party, who attempted to save the

Militärvorlage (Army Bill) in 1893 by proposing a more modest increase in the size of the army

[96] Jean-Louis Forain (1852–1931), French Impressionist artist

[97] Schoenaich-Carolath was a member of the Reichstag, but from this detail we learn that the interview took place at the Herrenhaus (House of Lords) of the Prussian Parliament in Berlin, where the prince was also a member.

[98] The manorial seigneur and former clergyman in *Rosmersholm* (1886) by Henrik Ibsen

[99] In 1878 the Province of Prussia (not to be confused with the far more extensive Kingdom of Prussia) was divided into East (with its capital in Königsberg, present-day Kaliningrad, Russia) and West (with its capital in Danzig, present-day Gdańsk, Poland).

[100] The Prussian House of Representatives was the lower house of the parliament of the Kingdom of Prussia

[101] Presumably Rudolf von Bennigsen (1824–1902), National Liberal member of the Reichstag

[102] His apartment was in a liberal stronghold; see note 12

[103] Satyr-like figure from Greek mythology associated with Dionysus

[104] Veteran of the pan-European rebellions in 1848

[105] Presumably a reference to works such as *In the Play of the Waves* (1883) by Swiss artists Arnold Böcklin (1827–1901), which depict old men gambolling lustily with mermaids

[106] Antisemites applied the disparaging term to both the Free-Minded Party and Mommsen's Association for Defence against Antisemitism, of which Rickert was a member.

[107] Present-day Mali Lošinj, Croatia, then a part of the Austro-Hungarian Empire

[108] Here Bahr draws a parallel (with presumably a measure of self-mockery) between his time in Paris and the adventures described in *Scènes de la vie de bohème* (1851), Henri Murger's highly influential and much-adapted novel of idealistic urban squalor in garrets, taverns and the Café Momus which defined bohemianism in the public imagination.

[109] The Exposition Universelle held in 1889 to mark the 100th anniversary of the French Revolution

[110] 'Helene', a romantic epic poem (1888), and the verse collections *Sturm* (Storm, 1888) and *Das starke Jahr* (The Strong Year, 1890), all early works by Mackay

[111] *L'Autonomie individuelle*, a French anarchist journal published in 1887–1888, mentioned approvingly in Mackay's *The Anarchists*

[112] Benjamin Tucker (1854–1939), founder of the anarchist journal *Liberty*

to which Mackay contributed

[113] The city's observatory at the time was near Hallesches Tor.

[114] An anthology of treatises published in 1888

[115] The German Society for Ethical Culture formed in 1892 by Foerster and Georg von Gizycki

[116] The movement associated with French war hero and early right-wing populist Georges Boulanger (1837–1891), which only turned antisemitic after his death by suicide

[117] Naquet was an outspoken supporter of marriage law reform, particularly concerning the right to legal dissolution; in 1877 he published a book entitled *Le Divorce*.

[118] The Austro-Hungarian Empire (if this is what Naquet is referring to) in fact emancipated the Jews in 1867.

[119] *La Libre Parole*, a journal which frequently published antisemitic material, established in 1892 by Édouard Drumont

[120] A French journalist and political figure who published the key antisemitic text *La France Juive* in 1886 and founded the Antisemitic League of France in 1889

[121] Francis Laur (1844–1934), French deputy who frequently alluded to scandals said to involve Jewish corruption and, as Naquet indicates, was influential in the antisemitic turn of the Boulangist faction

[122] Henri Meilhac (1830–1897), author of numerous stage works including *Margot* (1890) and librettist for the other two works mentioned, both operas by Jacques Offenbach

[123] Rudolf von Gneist (1816–1895), German politician and jurist. Bahr interviewed Gneist for his *Antisemitism* series; their encounter was published in the *Deutsche Zeitung* but for some reason excluded from the subsequent book publication.

[124] 'He was above all and before anything else a liberal and a moderate', from Ernest Daudet's 1883 pamphlet simply entitled *Jules Simon*

[125] The National Constituent Assembly, formed in the wake of the 1848 revolution

[126] Charles de Montalembert (1810–1870), Catholic politician whose liberal views put him at odds with the Ultramontanists (Catholics loyal to Vatican power)

[127] General Patrice de MacMahon, French President who succeeded Adolphe Thiers (1797–1877) who had become president following the fall of Emperor Napoleon III in 1870

[128] Henri Rochefort, another Bahr interviewee (although not in the original series of articles); Anne de Rochechouart de Mortemart, Duchess of Uzès, both an antisemite and a feminist, wealthy backer of General Boulanger

[129] General Gustave Paul Cluseret, Bahr interviewee

[130] 'a country of tolerance, if not indifference'

[131] The Paris Institute of Political Studies, the prestigious school now known as a breeding ground for France's political elite under the name Sciences Po

[132] The Academy of Moral and Political Sciences, a body of the Institut de France established in 1795

[133] In 1873 Paul Leroy-Beaulieu revived the journal, which had originally been founded by Jules Duval in 1862 but which had lain dormant since 1870.

[134] The Institut de France, which has operated since 1795 in a building originally established by Cardinal Mazarin as the Collège des Quatre-Nations

[135] Charles Perrault, the author of *Sleeping Beauty*, was an Academy member

[136] Adrien Albert Marie, Comte de Mun (1841–1914), politician whose views combined social consciousness with devout Catholicism and who later became a prominent anti-Dreyfusard; Prince Philippe, Comte de Paris (1838–1894), grandson of the last King of France

[137] **Author's footnote:** *Israël chez les nations.* Paris, Calmann-Lévy

[138] The old French administrative court; within a few years the ruins were cleared for the Gare (now Musée) d'Orsay

[139] Agénor Bardoux (1829–1897), minister responsible for education, arts and religion from 1877 to 1879: 'France does not live on the first floor, it lives on the third, or the fourth, sometimes under the roof' (quoted by Jules Claretie in *La vie à Paris*, 1881)

[140] An etching of prominent critic Edmond de Goncourt by Félix Bracquemond; Goncourt was a friend of Daudet and godfather to his daughter; he would die in Daudet's house in 1896.

[141] Eugène Carrière created at least two images of Daudet with his daughter Edmée around 1891.

[142] Jules Lemaître referred to Daudet's 'violent sensibility' in *Les contemporains* (Série 2, 1886).

[143] Author's footnote: Léon Daudet, philosopher poet of *Germe et Poussière*, is married to Jeanne Hugo, granddaughter of Victor Hugo.

[144] Writers' Society formed in 1838; Émile Zola had been president since 1891

[145] *Le Prince d'Aurec* (later known as *Les Descendants*), a satirical play written by Henri Lavedan (1859–1940) which depicted a confrontation between old French aristocracy and a wealthy Jewish businessman which became a great success although rejected by its intended venue, the Comédie-Française

[146] Daudet completed the novel *Soutien de famille* (The Pillar of the Family) shortly before his death in 1897 and it was published posthumously the following year; it appears that he never got to fashion the material into a drama as he had intended.

[147] Académie française; Magnard died around the time that Bahr's book appeared, and he was never elected to the august body.

[148] 'to give the readers one idea every day'

[149] 'the most interesting and interested minds of our time'; Catulle Mendès (1841–1909), French writer of Portuguese-Jewish extraction

[150] 'moral, social, artistic tightrope-walker'/'to satisfy every opinion, to please every party, to attract subscriptions from every camp' (Émile Bergerat)

[151] *La France Juive* (Jewish France, 1886), Drumont's influential antisemitic text

[152] This was an innovation introduced by Arthur Meyer in 1893 to create a greater bond between *Le Gaulois* and its readership, a physical space where they could view images and text related to current events and personalities and, as Bahr indicates, also hear live theatre performances (the *théâtrophone*) and phonograph records.

[153] Presumably Belgian Wagnerian tenor Ernest van Dyck (1861–1923); Bahr interviewed van Dyck as part of his series on theatre in Vienna.

[154] General Alfred-Amédée Dodds, hero of the Franco-Prussian War

[155] This refers to a still-fresh story in the Parisian press concerning an anarchist prank pulled by Achille Le Roy, a veteran of the Commune, who nominated himself for the Académie française; dressed in the uniform of a Bolivian general, he delivered his 'application' to the Académie in a kettle, a reference to a recent incident in which the anarchist Ravachol had deployed a home-made bomb fashioned from such a utensil. Once the trio returned to the Left Bank they were met with cries of 'Vive Le Roy!'. The photo to which Bahr refers is a parody of the formal portraiture of the time which shows Le Roy flanked by fellow agitators Maxime Lisbonne and Marius Tournadre, with the caption '*Les trois académicides*'.

[156] The time in the early evening favoured for drinking absinthe

[157] Gabriel Terrail, journalist who wrote under the name 'Mermeix' (and had recently written a book about antisemitism); Émile de Girardin, journalist who had died in 1881; Marcel Hirsch, also known as Marcel Hutin, reporter at *Le Gaulois*

[158] minion

[159] *Le Monde où l'on s'ennuie* (1868, translated as *The Art of Being Bored*), *La Souris* (1887, The Mouse) and *L'Étincelle* (1879, The Spark), popular stage comedies by Pailleron

[160] Henry Fouquier (1838–1901), French journalist

[161] *'faire l'école buissonnière'* – to skip school

[162] French anarchist and key figure of the Paris Commune

[163] Jules Vallès (1832–1885), French writer and key influence on Séverine and her writing career

[164] Séverine's first husband is recorded as Antoine-Henri Montrobert

[165] Adrien Guébhard (1848–1924), Swiss-French writer

[166] Daily newspaper originally founded by Jules Vallès shortly before the Paris Commune in 1871 and relaunched in 1883

[167] Stanislas Padlewski was a Polish revolutionary who assassinated a former head of the Russian secret police in Paris in 1890. Padlewski's supporters engaged Séverine's assistance, and she in turn convinced Georges de Labruyère to help him escape over the Italian border. Padlewski eventually made his way to the United States, but in despair over his situation he committed suicide in San Antonio in 1891.

[168] At a gathering of Boulangists in 1888, an impatient Séverine apparently tore off the red carnation she was wearing in her button hole and flung it on the table with the words, 'There you go, that's your emblem! Redder than a Cocarde!' This single impetuous gesture evidently supplied both the floral symbol for the movement and the name for *La Cocarde*, the Boulangist daily newspaper founded by Georges de Labruyère.

[169] Séverine was, as Bahr indicates, a frequent subject for artists, although there is no record of a Marie Coutant, and the Renouard of Bahr's text is presumably not the artist Paul Renouard but a mishearing of (Auguste) Renoir, who executed the most famous portrait of the writer (1885, now held in the National Gallery of Art in Washington, DC) as well as a number of works on paper. Louise Abbéma was a prominent artist of the Belle Époque, and is thought to have painted Séverine around the time of this interview. The portrait by Amélie Beaury-Saurel (1848–1924) was exhibited in the 1893 Salon de la Société des artistes français, and is now held by the Musée Carnavalet in Paris.

[170] François Coppée (1842–1908), French writer, in the poem 'Pour Élise Duguéret' ('a woman with a big heart, the good Séverine'), dedicated to the tragic actress mentioned earlier as a beneficiary of Séverine's largesse

[171] 'annoy the government'

[172] Drumont's pamphlet (1892) referred to an incident that occurred on May Day, 1891, in which government forces launched a deadly attack on unarmed strikers in Fourmies; Drumont held Jewish officials accountable.

[173] *Littérature de tout à l'heure* (Literature of Today, 1889), a key text on the Symbolist movement

[174] *Kreisleriana*, a series of works by German Romantic writer E. T. A.

Hoffmann featuring the character Johannes Kreisler

[175] On the Religious Meaning of Poetry, 1893

[176] The 'July Revolution' of 1830 brought down Charles XII, the last Bourbon king, and ushered in the Orléanist Louis-Philippe.

[177] Blidah, Algeria, where Cluseret took part in the French conquest of the Kabylie region in 1857

[178] Garibaldi and his army laid siege to Capua in October 1860 during the Second War of Italian Independence; Cluseret was wounded during the battle.

[179] Prince Robert d'Orléans, Duke of Chartres, and his brother Prince Philippe d'Orleans, Comte de Paris, grandsons of the last king of France, fought in the Army of the Potomac commanded by General George B. McClellan.

[180] The short-lived *New Nation* newspaper, established by Frémont in 1864 to aid his presidential campaign, favoured expansion of democracy and opposed Abraham Lincoln; it was an early example of a politician deploying an entire media outlet for his own ends.

[181] In 1867, the Irish Republican organisation, the Fenian Brotherhood, organised a revolt (the 'Fenian Rising') in County Kerry and Dublin, followed by terrorist attacks in England.

[182] The 1867 Fenian raid on Chester Castle aimed to secure arms kept there; Aulif sometimes also rendered as 'Auliff'.

[183] Prison in Paris

[184] The revolution that brought about the fall of the Second Empire following France's defeat in the Battle of Sedan during the Franco-Prussian War, ushering in the Government of National Defence and the Third Republic

[185] This failed rebellion in Lyon mirrored events in Paris and also led to the establishment of a Commune in which Cluseret fought alongside the anarchist Mikhail Bakunin (or in the words of an unimpressed Karl Marx, 'Bakunin and Cluseret arrived at Lyons and spoiled everything'); in a similar uprising in Marseilles, Cluseret was named Commander of the National Guard (presumably this is the title behind Bahr's reference to a 'Marshal of southern France').

[186] Another prison in Paris

[187] The 'Bloody Week' of 21–28 May signalled the end of the Commune as the French army loyal to Adolphe Thiers (not German troops, as Bahr avers) fought the Communards in heavy street-to-street combat.

[188] Cluseret was condemned to death in absentia by the Military Tribunal of Satory (Versailles).

[189] Arch-bohemian Rodolphe Salis (1851–1897)

[190] Rafael von Ambros (1855–1895), Austrian painter of Egyptian street scenes

[191] Marius Michel (1853–1910), French painter

[192] Ludwig Gabillon (1825–1896), prominent Austrian stage actor

[193] József Bem (1794–1850), György Klapka (1820–1892), Lajos Kossuth (1802–1894), Ferenc Pulszky (1814–1897), all figures associated with the Hungarian independence movement

[194] Pilar Cuevas y Bringas, wife of the Marqués de Alta Villa and lady-in-waiting to the exiled Queen Isabella

[195] Rachilde (Marguerite Vallette-Eymery, 1860–1953), French Decadent writer of *La Marquise de Sade*, *Monsieur Vénus* and other provocative works, and hostess of a long-running salon

[196] Paul Mounet (1847–1922), French actor; Ludwig Martinelli (1832–1913), Austrian actor

[197] Ignacio Bauer (1828–1895), Spanish banker of Hungarian-Jewish origins

[198] Part of the 'Glorious Revolution', the Battle of Alcolea on a bridge over the River Guadalquivir, in which General Francisco Serrano, in league with Juan Prim, led his troops to victory against forces loyal to the queen, Isabella II

[199] The uprising that first forced Zorrilla's exile to Paris, from which he returned in 1868

[200] Alfonso XII (1857–1885), King of Spain, Duke of Montpensier (1824–1890), Ferdinand II of Portugal (1816–1885), Luís of Portugal (1838–1889); Prince Tommaso of Savoy, Duke of Genoa (1854–1931; he was just 13 at the time) were considered as potential successors to the Spanish throne.

[201] Amadeo I (1845–1890), son of Vittorio Emanuele II of Italy, King of Spain 1870–1873

[202] Antonio Cánovas del Castillo (1828–1897) who became Prime Minister following the coup against the republic by General Martínez Campos (1831–1900)

[203] Newspaper launched by Rochefort in 1868 after his dismissal from *Le Figaro*

[204] Édouard Ducret (1854–1900), right-wing journalist who made accusations that Georges Clemenceau was in league with the British, and Boulangist politician Lucien Millevoye (1850–1918) who presented documents to the Chamber of Deputies that he claimed supported the accusation; *gobeur* refers to someone who is gullible.

[205] Rochefort was initially detained in the prison of Saint-Pierre in Versailles for his seditious writings, then to a series of fortress prisons including Saint-Martin-de-Ré, and finally banished to New Caledonia,

from where he escaped to Australia in 1874 with the assistance of Freemasons.

[206] 'At once one of the most interesting and most irritating moral cases due to the impossibility of seeing all the way down to the bottom'

[207] 'I can summon two hundred thousand men from the outskirts whenever I want' (a *manieur d'hommes* is a people handler)

[208] Jan van Beers (1852–1927), date of the portrait unknown

[209] Adolphe Crémieux (1796–1880), member of the Government of National Defence, which extended citizenship to Jews in Algeria, then a colony of France, but not to the Muslim majority

[210] The Rothschilds were accused of complicity in the collapse of the French copper market in 1889.

[211] The royal dynasty began in 1818 when Napoleon appointed one of his marshals, Jean Bernadotte, to the Swedish throne; an extremely tenuous rumour held that Bernadotte was part Jewish.

[212] Baron Frédéric Spitzer (1815–1890), collector and dealer in artworks, whose collection of over 4,000 items, largely Renaissance and medieval, was auctioned in 1893. Some of the works were later found to be forgeries.

[213] Ferdinand de Lesseps (1805–1894), French diplomat behind the ill-fated first Panama Canal scheme

[214] All three generations were named Charles Wentworth Dilke; the interviewee's father, generally known as Wentworth Dilke, helped to organise the 1851 Great Exhibition; his grandfather, co-owner of the *Athenaeum*, was generally known as Charles Wentworth Dilke. Charles Dickens was the co-founder and first editor of the *Daily News*.

[215] Dilke's 1874 satire about a dethroned prince who 'happens to be a republican'

[216] Whitechapel had attracted Jewish immigrants from the Russian Empire, mostly from poor rural areas, following the pogroms of the 1880s. This area of London's East End was noted at the time for its poverty and squalor.

[217] Original in English

[218] Charles Bradlaugh (1833–1891), British parliamentarian, republican and founder of Britain's National Secular Society

[219] Newspaper founded by Labouchère in 1877 which aimed at uncovering corruption; it lasted in various forms until 1957.

[220] Russian-born Madame (Helena) Blavatsky (1831–1891) was a spiritual figure whose teachings exerted an immense influence throughout the world in the 19th century; in 1875 she founded the Theosophical Society which drew from Western esotericism, Eastern mysticism and classical

philosophy.

[221] This presumably refers to French occultist Gérard Encausse (known as Papus) who left the Theosophical Society in 1890 and went on to join the Rosicrucian revival.

[222] German artist Hermann Schmiechen (1855–1925) painted Blavatsky (two separate portraits, 1884, 1885) as well as other leading members of the Theosophical movement.

[223] Karl Hillebrand (1829–1884), polyglot German writer who spanned European nations in his series *Zeiten, Völker und Menschen* (Eras, Nations and People); Georg Brandes (1842–1927), influential Danish critic; Juan Valera y Alcalá-Galiano (1824–1905), widely travelled Spanish writer and diplomat

[224] Franz von Lenbach (1836–1904) was a friend of Whitman, who would later dedicate his book *Personal Reminiscences of Prince Bismarck* (1902) to the German artist.

[225] Helmut von Moltke (1848–1916), German military commander and aide-de-camp to Kaiser Wilhelm II

[226] 'The Anti-Semitic Movement' in *The Contemporary Review*, May 1893, which abounds with antisemitic tropes, and even rebukes Jews for 'blackening of the character of the Anti-Semitic leaders'

[227] German stage actor (1815–1888) who was captured by Josef Fux in a portrait showing him in the role of Vanssen in Goethe's *Egmont*

[228] Major embezzlement case in 1876 concerning Eugène T'Kindt of the Banque de Belgique; criminal trial of the Peltzer brothers, Léon and Armand, who murdered a prominent lawyer in 1882

[229] Belgian writer Camille Lemonnier (1844–1913), who often ran into trouble with the authorities for 'indecent' writings, was tried for the story 'L'Enfant du crapaud' which appeared in the Parisian journal *Gil Blas* in 1888. Picard defended Lemonnier by referencing his particularly 'Belgian temperament', but a fine of 1000 francs was upheld.

[230] A vast series that would eventually encompass over 150 volumes covering every aspect of Belgian law

[231] Maurice Maeterlinck (1862–1949), Belgian writer chiefly associated with Symbolism

[232] *Journal des Tribunaux*, Belgian legal journal founded by Picard in 1888 which continues to this day; *L'Art moderne. Revue critique des Arts et de la Littérature* launched by Picard in 1881 and continuing until 1914

[233] Synthesis of Antisemitism (1892)

[234] Count André Langrand-Dumonceau (1826–1900) was a Belgian financier who in his campaign to 'Christianise' capital sought to combat what he regarded as Jewish domination of banking through strong Catholic competition. He had notable backers, including the King of

Belgium and Pope Pius IX, but his investment plans were actually something like a present-day Ponzi scheme, and his financial empire collapsed in 1870.

[235] Present-day Oslo

[236] In parallel with Bahr's series of interviews in the *Deutsche Zeitung* in 1893, articles featuring three leading Italian scientists discussing the current state of antisemitism in their country appeared in the rival *Neue Freie Presse*. These were not in the interview style established by Bahr, instead they were lengthy first-person essays outlining the views of the respective respondents. They were Cesare Lombroso (1835–1909), physician, psychiatrist and criminologist and the only Jew of the trio, Enrico Ferri (1856–1929), also a criminologist and Paolo Mantegazza (1831–1910), neurologist and writer.

INTERVIEWEES

Bahr's 38 interviewees represented seven western European nationalities – German (14), French (11), English (5), Belgian (3), Spanish (2), Norwegian (2) and Irish (1). Surprisingly, considering the author's nationality and the interviews' original publication in a Viennese newspaper, there were no Austrians. Only two respondents were women (Séverine, Annie Besant) and only three were Jewish (Maximilian Harden, Alfred Naquet, Arthur Meyer). The average age of the interviewees was 53. The oldest respondent was half a century older than the youngest; Jules Simon's birth coincided with Napoleon's exile on Elba while John Henry Mackay was around the same age as Bahr, born during the American Civil War and still in his twenties when he reunited with Bahr for their interview. Aside from Mackay, the respondents with whom Bahr was known to have had personal contact prior to their respective interviews were Theodor Barth, August Bebel, Gustav Schmoller, Adolph Wagner, Alejandro Sawa and Henrik Ibsen. In the original he addresses Sawa and Mackay – the two youngest respondents and also friends of the writer – with the familiar *du* form; for everyone else he uses the formal *Sie*. Eight of the interviewees submitted their responses in writing – Foerster, Pailleron, Balfour, Labouchère, Ibsen, Bjørnson, Egidy and Schmeidler, although Bahr did also visit the latter two.

Several interviewees had multiple occupations (with a number combining politics and writing, for instance), but if we examine their primary roles, we find one jurist, two scientists, two historians, two economists and three spiritual figures, with the rest almost evenly divided between writers and politicians – 13 and 14 respectively. This only leaves Cluseret – the effectively uncategorisable mercenary of revolution turned amateur artist.

The names used throughout reflect present usage. In the original, Bahr transliterated some names ('Manuel Ruy Zorilla', 'Björnsterne Björnson'), reordered others ('James Arthur Balfour' instead of Arthur James Balfour, more commonly Arthur Balfour), and curiously referred to Gustave Paul Cluseret and Charles Buls solely by their surnames.

Arthur Balfour (1848–1930) was born to a political dynasty and elected to parliament as a Conservative member in 1869. His further rise was evidently aided by (literal) nepotism, as Balfour received a number of important posts under his uncle, Lord Salisbury, who was first Foreign Secretary then Prime Minister. Balfour himself was appointed Secretary for Ireland, then Leader of the House of Commons. By the time he spoke to Bahr he was in opposition, but returned to the role of Leader of the Commons in 1895. In 1902, Balfour succeeded his uncle as Prime Minister, resigning in 1905. He remained active in parliament and later became Foreign Secretary. It was in this post that he would come to exert a greater influence on Jewish life than any other respondent thanks to a 1917 letter that became known as the 'Balfour Declaration', which outlined the principle of a Jewish homeland in Palestine.

German politician **Theodor Barth** (1849–1909) served in the Reichstag, on and off, from 1881 to 1898, and thereafter in the Prussian parliament. Trained as a lawyer, he first came to public attention as an opponent of Bismarck's protectionist policies. Throughout his political career he moved about the liberal spectrum, initially favouring unhindered market forces before gravitating to a position closer to the Social Democrats, as reflected in his discussion with Bahr. Barth's negative comments about Eugen Richter, who was head of the Free-Minded Party of which Barth was a member at the time, prefigure the schism that occurred just weeks after this interview; Barth joined one offshoot of the party, with its rival headed by Richter. Barth was a member of Theodor Mommsen's Association for Defence against Antisemitism.

August Bebel (1840–1913) was the key parliamentary representative of German left-wing thinking in the late 19th century and the founder of the country's Social Democrat movement that continues as a major force in Germany's political life to this day. In 1867 he became a member of the Reichstag (of the North German Confederation, initially, and from 1871 the empire) and served until his death. The rise of the Social Democrats alarmed Bismarck who first banned left-wing parties, and then partly co-opted their methods, by adopting a measure of social welfare. Bebel consistently battled militarism, colonialism, subjugation of women and other repressive remnants of the old order.

Annie Besant (1847–1933) was an outspoken supporter of a wide range of positions – political, social and spiritual – that placed her at odds with the British mainstream of her time. She was involved with the National Secular Society and the Fabian Society and took part in a violent demonstration in London against conditions in Ireland. In 1890 she met Madame Blavatsky and joined her Theosophical Society. On behalf of the group she travelled to India, beginning a long association with the sub-continent. In 1907 she assumed the presidency of the Theosophical Society, based in Madras, and became active in Indian politics, and a supporter of the country's independence movement.

Norwegian writer **Bjørnstjerne Bjørnson** (1832–1910) was involved with almost every aspect of his country's literary life and politics. His varied writings ranged from early novels set among the peasantry to poetic and dramatic pieces of ambitious scope that drew on earlier Norwegian traditions, as well as journalism reflecting his left-wing politics. A frequent visitor to France, Bjørnson would become a passionate defender of Alfred Dreyfus. Bjørnson was one of the first recipients of the Nobel Prize for Literature, issued when he himself was serving on the Norwegian Nobel Committee.

Charles (also known as Karel) **Buls** (1837–1914) was a Belgian politician who served as the Mayor of Brussels for much of the last two decades of the 19th century, during which time he was also active at the national level in the Chamber of Representatives. His efforts to preserve the architectural heritage of Brussels brought him into conflict with King Leopold II, who had more ambitious plans for his capital. Buls published a number of works on urban planning as well as travel reports.

Gustave Paul Cluseret (1823–1900) was a larger-than-life figure who threw himself into uprisings in several countries. After serving in a battalion that helped suppress the

1848 rebellion in Paris, taking part in the Crimean War and aiding the fight for Italian unification, he headed to the US, where he joined the Civil War on the Union side alongside John C. Frémont. Afterward, Cluseret joined Frémont's campaign to become the first Republican president, and the two men together launched the *New Nation* newspaper in New York. Cluseret subsequently aligned himself with the radical Irish Fenian movement and was involved in the British Reform League. He joined the Communards after the fall of Napoleon III, becoming Delegate for War. After the Commune fell, Cluseret fled the country, spending time in Constantinople and returning to become a Deputy in 1888. As his interview with Bahr reflects, he espoused antisemitic views late in life.

French novelist **Alphonse Daudet** (1840–1897) was largely associated with Naturalism. His most acclaimed novel was *Tartarin of Tarascon* (1872) which drew on his childhood in Provence and spawned two further books featuring the same titular character. Among his other works are the novels *Les Rois en exil* and *L'Évangéliste*, and the drama *L'Arlésienne*. The syphilitic illness already in evidence in his encounter with Bahr claimed his life just a few years later. The interview also captured his quixotic opinions, although he was certainly known for antisemitic, anti-republican views among his contemporaries. His novels were widely read in his lifetime and remain popular in France to this day.

British politician **Sir Charles Dilke** (1843–1911) became a Member of Parliament in the Liberal party in 1868 and rose to prominence in government, including a position on the Privy Council. He was associated with a number of progressive causes of the time, such as universal suffrage, workers' rights and republicanism. His further rise was checked by a messy and highly public divorce case in which he stood accused of affairs with a mother and daughter. He lost his seat in parliament in 1886 and gained another in 1892.

Born in Mainz to a long-established Saxon aristocratic line, **Moritz von Egidy** (1847–1898) enrolled early on as a cadet and in 1866 fought in the Prussian army against Austria, later transferring to the Saxon army. There he attained the rank of lieutenant colonel but was forced to leave the army following the 1890 publication of his book *Ernste Gedanken* (Serious Thoughts) which called for a revival of Christianity that rejected narrow denominational confines while emphasising love and a direct connection with God. He was highly influential in late 19th-century Germany.

Wilhelm Foerster (1832–1921) was Professor of Astronomy at the University of Berlin and director of the Berlin Observatory for almost forty years. He was also influential in helping establish international standards for weights and measures. Foerster was engaged with the issues of his day, as witnessed by his role in the founding of the German Society for Ethical Culture (with philosopher Georg von Gizycki), and his membership of the German Peace Society as well as Mommsen's Association for Defence against Antisemitism. While the original Berlin Observatory no longer stands, its replacement now bears his name.

Polymath **Ernst Haeckel** (1834–1919) was one of the most prominent and respected scientific minds of 19th-century Germany, his work building on Darwinian evolution, with his richly illustrated volumes making complex biological phenomena accessible to lay readers. His interests extended far beyond natural history, and he was a key figure of modern Monism as well as a proponent of social Darwinism and the pseudo-science of 'racial hygiene'. Although he travelled extensively he is most readily associated with the Thuringian city of Jena, where much of his academic career played out; he held the chair of Zoology at the University of Jena for almost half a century.

Maximilian Harden (1861–1927) was the most prominent and contentious journalistic voice of the Wilhelmine era. Born as Felix Witkoswski to a middle-class Jewish family in Berlin, he converted to Protestantism in 1878 and adopted his best-known pseudonym. By that time he was already a jobbing actor, first making a name for himself as a journalist in 1884. He was highly influential in German theatre, a key force in the formation of the Freie Bühne and the Deutsches Theater. In 1892 he established *Die Zukunft*, a weekly which offered stern opposition to the follies of Wilhelm II. He was the instigator of the major scandal of pre-World War One Germany, the Harden-Eulenburg Affair, in which he claimed the Kaiser was surrounded by a homosexual cabal. He almost died in a right-wing extremist attack after the war, although he survived for a further five years.

Politician and lawyer **Tim Healy** (1855–1931) was born in Ireland in modest circumstances and retained a great interest in the cause of Irish independence after he moved to England as a young man, expressed in articles for *The Nation* newspaper. In 1880 Healy was elected to parliament for the Irish Parliamentary Party, and was initially a great supporter of the party's head, Charles Parnell, before they fell out in 1890, with Healy joining a breakaway group after Parnell's death the following year. Healy's ensuing on-off political career ran in parallel with a successful legal practice. He became a key figure in Ireland's transition to nationhood in 1922 when he was appointed Governor-General of the newly created Irish

Free State, a position he retained until 1928.

Norwegian playwright **Henrik Ibsen** (1828–1906) exerted near incalculable influence in his time and remains the most performed dramatist after Shakespeare to this day. Having initially studied chemistry, Ibsen saw his first work staged in 1850 and his ensuing oeuvre spans the entire second half of the 19th century. While initial plays were unsuccessful, he was active in theatres in Bergen and Christiania (Oslo). His breakthrough works were *Brand* (1865) and *Peer Gynt* (1867). Ibsen spent a good deal of his later career in Germany and Italy. His later works such as *Hedda Gabler* and *A Doll's House* were extremely critical of societal mores, particularly the treatment of women. With respect to Bahr's enquiry, it should be noted that Norway's Jewish population was almost non-existent, with Oslo's first community only formally established in 1892.

Belgian politician **Paul Janson** (1840–1913) first made his name as a trainee lawyer in the 'De Buck Affair' in which Jesuit orders were accused of impropriety in dealing with legacies of deceased estates. Janson launched his parliamentary career for the Belgian Liberal Party in 1877. Returning to the Chamber of Representatives after a few years' absence, he took up the cause of universal (male) suffrage, which was introduced in 1893. He lost his seat the following year, regaining it in 1900 and holding it until his death. He was the patriarch of a political dynasty active in Belgium well into the 20th century.

Henry Labouchère (1831–1912) was born to a wealthy English family with French Huguenot roots. While still a young man he achieved a number of postings in the diplomatic corps, in Washington and various European capitals. In 1867 he became a member of parliament, although he lost his seat the following year. Labouchère then became a theatre impresario and journalist, founding his own scandalous journal *Truth* in 1877. His dismissive response to Bahr notwithstanding, Labouchère was known to be deeply antisemitic, and attacked Jewish figures in print. He was re-elected to parliament in 1880. His scurrilous journalism, whose targets included the royal family, came back to haunt him when, as Bahr notes, Queen Victoria personally stepped in to prevent his further ascent. After a later controversy in which he evidently enriched himself by using *Truth* to manipulate share prices, he retired to Italy.

Anatole Leroy-Beaulieu (1842–1912) was a French writer and historian particularly concerned with Russia, on which he was considered an authority. In 1881 Leroy-Beaulieu became professor of contemporary history and Oriental affairs at the elite École libre des sciences politiques, becoming the director of the school in 1906. He was an outspoken opponent of antisemitism, publishing *Israël chez les nations,* (1883) and *L'Antisémitisme* (1897) as well as a 1905 study of Jewish immigrants in the United States. Leroy-Beaulieu was equally opposed to anti-clericalism and other anti-religious sentiment, forming the National League Against Atheism in 1901. His brother Paul was a noted economist.

Although born in Scotland, writer **John Henry Mackay** (1864–1933) spent all but his earliest infancy in Germany. He was one of the country's most prominent advocates of individualist anarchy, and wrote a biography of the movement's founder, Max Stirner. His breakthrough as a writer came in 1891 with *Die Anarchisten* (The Anarchists) which espoused Stirner's principles and compared them favourably to communist anarchism while also considering the role of violence in self-actualisation. Mackay additionally issued poetry along with a number of books that expressed his attraction to male adolescents with unusual frankness, both under his own name and the pseudonym Sagitta. His influence, in political matters at least, extended well beyond Germany.

Little remembered now, **Francis Magnard** (1837–1894) was a widely-read journalist of his time. He was associated with *Le Figaro* throughout his career, joining the newspaper in 1865 and becoming editor-in-chief in 1876 and co-owner in 1879, with considerable success. All the while Magnard continued to write for a number of other publications. He published two novels, *L'Abbé Jérôme* (1869) and *Vie et aventures d'un positiviste, histoire paradoxale* (1876). Magnard died around the time that Bahr's book appeared.

French journalist and newspaper owner **Arthur Meyer** (1844–1924) was chiefly known as the proprietor of *Le Gaulois*, a newspaper with a relatively small but highly influential readership, a conservative voice which nonetheless found room for writers such as J. K. Huysmans, Colette and Octave Mirbeau. As the text indicates, Meyer was highly innovative in engaging reader interest with methods including waxworks of contemporary figures and the newsroom described by Bahr. Although he was a Catholic convert, Meyer's Jewish origins made him a target for antisemites such as Édouard Drumont, who referred to him disparagingly in his book *La France Juive*, prompting a duel between the two men. *Le Gaulois* was absorbed into *Le Figaro* a few months after Meyer's death.

German historian **Theodor Mommsen** (1817–1903) was one of the most esteemed scholars of his day as well as a politician, first in the Prussian parliament, and then the Reichstag. A liberal, he combined passionate patriotism with strident opposition to antisemitism. Around 1880 he was involved in a major public dispute when he sharply criticised an essay by fellow historian Heinrich von Treitschke which popularised the term *Antisemitismus*. Mommsen formed the Association for Defence against Antisemitism in 1890. In 1902 he won the Nobel Prize in Literature for his *A History of Rome*, a subject on which he was a widely acknowledged authority.

Charles Morice (1860–1919) was an essayist, poet and translator who was chiefly associated with Symbolism. He wrote about the movement for *Lutèce* and *La Revue contemporaine*, and was on friendly terms with a number of its leading figures, although his friendship with Paul Verlaine was preceded by a public spat. Morice synthesised the aims of Symbolism in his major work, *La Littérature de tout à l'heure* (1889). He was also instrumental in translating and popularising Dostoyevsky in French. Morice only published his own poetry in the 20th century, and at times was forced to support his literary endeavours by working as a shipping clerk and a school teacher.

Alfred Naquet (1834–1916) was a French-Jewish professor of chemistry who found early notoriety when he was jailed for membership in a seditious society and conspiracy to supply explosives. He was later part of an organisation headed by anarchist Mikhail Bakunin. His parliamentary career began in 1871; in 1889 he was a deputy for the faction aligned with right-wing war hero and populist General Boulanger, a group that became openly antisemitic after Boulanger's death in 1891. As a prominent Jew he was a target for increasing antisemitism, and was accused of corruption as part of the Panama Scandal, although finally acquitted. He was noted as an outspoken advocate of legalised divorce.

Writer **Edouard Pailleron** (1834–1899) lived his entire life in Paris. He was still a young man when he became co-director of the influential *Revue des Deux Mondes*, which was owned by his father-in-law. His greatest success came with the 1881 satirical stage comedy *Le Monde où l'on s'ennuie* (translated as *The Art of Being Bored*). Pailleron was elected to the Académie francaise. The writer, his wife and children were subjects of a number of paintings by John Singer Sargent, a family friend.

Edmond Picard (1836–1924) was one of the most prominent Belgian legal minds of his time, and published extensively on juridical matters, while also serving in parliament as a socialist senator. He was alert to contemporary currents in arts and letters and issued his own literary works. Picard was also responsible for a number of incendiary polemical writings that reflected his overt racism, introducing virulent political antisemitism to a country that was otherwise largely free of it.

German journalist and politician **Heinrich Rickert** (1833–1902) started out in Königsberg (now Kaliningrad) and served in both the lower house of the Prussian Parliament and the Reichstag. He was a key figure of the National Liberal Party until he broke away in 1880 and formed his own Liberal Union, later absorbed into the Free-Minded Party. He was also editor of the *Danziger Zeitung*. Rickert was a supporter of women's emancipation, and women's right to study, and an opponent of antisemitism, joining Mommsen's Association for Defence against Antisemitism.

Henri Rochefort (1833–1913) was a confrontational, controversial French politician and journalist known for his extremist views which combined elements of both right- and left-wing thinking. Like his father, from whom he inherited an uncertain aristocratic title, Rochefort wrote for vaudeville. In 1863 he joined *Le Figaro* where he earned a reputation for his deliberately provocative texts, and on his dismissal started his own paper, *La Lanterne*, but after confrontation with the authorities he was forced to publish in Brussels and sell it clandestinely in France. Rochefort was a bitter opponent of Napoleon III's regime and joined the Commune in 1871. In the wake of its failure he was exiled to New Caledonia but escaped to the United States, only returning to France during an amnesty in 1880. Later in the decade he threw his lot in with General Boulanger, accompanying him to his exile in London. After his return to Paris in 1895 Rochefort became a passionate anti-Dreyfusard.

Spanish politician **Manuel Ruiz Zorrilla** (1833–1895) played a leading role in his country's public life in the second half of the 19th century. His parliamentary career began in 1856, but ten years later his association with seditious elements forced his exile from Spain. He returned after the 'Glorious Revolution' of 1868 and rose to the prime ministership on two separate occasions until the abdication of King Amadeo in 1873. Ruiz Zorrilla went into exile again in 1875 and in Paris he was a consistent voice of opposition to Alfonso XII and supporter of the republican cause. In 1895 he returned to Spain already gravely ill and died in Burgos.

Spanish writer **Alejandro Sawa** (1862–1909) lived an intensively bohemian existence in Madrid before moving to Paris in 1889 at a time of increased exchange between the respective avant-gardes in Spain and France. It was here that he first came into contact with Hermann Bahr as well as other literary figures both French and foreign. He produced a series of novels throughout the 1880s that were aligned with the Naturalist movement, including *La mujer de todo el mundo* and *Crimen legal*. His last years were dominated by the decline of his sight and mental faculties, and he was just 46 when he died.

Pastor J. (Johannes) **Schmeidler** (1841–1902) was a German theologian, signatory to Mommsen's 1880 declaration of opposition to antisemitism and fellow member of the Association for Defence against Antisemitism. Little more is known about him, other than that he was a leading figure in the Protestantenverein (Protestant Association).

Prominent economist **Gustav Schmoller** (1838–1917), later Gustav von Schmoller, was an influential figure well beyond his native Germany, where he numbered among the left-wing academics disparagingly referred to as *Kathedersozialisten*. His emphasis on social reform in economic theory placed him in opposition to both the radical free-market policies known in Germany as *Manchestertum*, and to revolutionary Marxism. Schmoller's interdisciplinary approach incorporated elements of sociology, constitutional law and administrative practice, and his interest in shaping policy led him to take a seat in the upper house of Prussia's parliament. It was in the mid-1880s that Bahr first encountered Schmoller, attending his lectures at the Friedrich Wilhelm University in Berlin.

As a young man, **Prince Heinrich zu Schoenaich-Carolath** (1852–1920) took part in the Franco-Prussian War, turning to politics upon leaving the army. In 1877 he became Councillor of the district of Guben and entered the Reichstag in 1881 as a member of the Free Conservative Party, joining the National Liberal Party in 1890. Hereditary privileges also brought him a seat in the upper house of Prussia's parliament. Despite his aristocratic background, Schoenaich-Carolath supported numerous progressive causes, including social welfare, female emancipation and equality between Jews and Gentiles, earning him the title of 'Red Prince'.

Caroline Rémy (1855–1929) was a prominent French

journalist and supporter of progressive movements who wrote under the name **Séverine**. It was after meeting leftist writer Jules Vallès in 1879 that she turned to journalism herself. In 1883 the pair revived the dormant newspaper *Le Cri du peuple*, while Séverine was also a highly prolific contributor to other publications. She championed numerous causes both in her writing and through direct activism, becoming an outspoken advocate for female suffrage and opponent of the antisemitism that attended the Dreyfus Affair. Her sympathy for radical movements extended to communism, even anarchy.

Born during the Napoleonic era, philosopher and politician **Jules Simon** (1814–1896) was the oldest of Bahr's interviewees. He entered the national parliament in the wake of the 1848 rebellion, but his opposition to the ensuing Second Empire regime hampered both his academic and political careers. He returned to parliament in 1863 and was a key figure in both the provisional government during the Franco-Prussian War and the subsequent Third Republic, serving as Education Minister. In 1875 he was elected to the hugely prestigious Académie française and became a senator for life. He was the author of numerous works on aspects of society, labour and administration.

In his youth **Friedrich Spielhagen** (1829–1911) witnessed the 1848 revolt in Berlin and was generally regarded as a liberal, and in 1859 became editor of the *Zeitung für Norddeutschland*, a democratically inclined newspaper. As well as journalism, his output encompassed numerous literary works and translations from English and French, his breakthrough coming with the 1861 novel *Problematische Naturen*, published in four volumes. The most acclaimed of his 20 or so novels, *Sturmflut*, came in 1877, by which time Spielhagen was a major figure of German letters. Later in life he drifted even further to the left, as his comments to Bahr foretell.

Adolph Wagner (1835–1917) was a highly influential and disputatious economist throughout the German Empire. Initially preoccupied with banking, his later writings were more concerned with the obligations of the state in the welfare of its citizens, and like Schmoller he was termed a *Kathedersozialist*, although he was also in favour of the monarchy. His economic theories resonated loudly in the Bismarck era as the Chancellor introduced a precursor to the modern welfare state, and retain much of their relevance to this day. Wagner was closely aligned with influential antisemite Adolf Stoecker.

A British writer of German extraction on his father's side, **Sidney Whitman** (1848–1925) received four years' schooling in Dresden which left him with mastery of German, a rarity among educated Englishmen of the time. A great enthusiast for German culture and politics, he first met the retired Otto von Bismarck in 1891 and on numerous occasions thereafter, and arrived at his estate one day in 1898 for what was to be another meeting to discover the Iron Chancellor had died in the night. Whitman enlightened his compatriots in matters concerning Germany and other parts of the continent in such books as *Imperial Germany, Personal Reminiscences of Prince Bismarck* and *The Realm of the Habsburgs*.

AFTERWORD

A document from the eve of the 20th century recording the views of leading figures in politics, journalism and literature across Europe would, you might think, be of great historical interest. Were that document to offer unguarded first-hand opinion on the most contentious issue of its time, capturing the rise of a violent, divisive force within society approaching its provisional apex, a force that would have harrowing resonance within decades and lasting impact to the present day, it would surely be of profound consequence. This is what we have before us in *Der Antisemitismus: Ein internationales Interview* (Antisemitism: An International Interview) by Austrian author Hermann Bahr, which recorded his discussions on the subject with public figures which appeared in newspaper articles throughout 1893, and as a book the following year.

For the 'Jewish question' was the most hotly debated issue in 1890s Europe, and the forms in which Bahr encounters it were of recent derivation; the term 'antisemitism' itself had only been in usage for little more than a decade. Bahr and his respondents make reference to numerous figures and events of the time that would have been familiar to au courant contemporaries but require a good deal of context for the reader of today. Yet there is little attention given to the sorry, centuries-long saga of anti-Jewish hatred in Europe with its pogroms, expulsions, forced conversions, ghettoes and inquisitions, with its tropes of blood libel, deicide, usury, rootlessness and treachery.

For a short while, in fact, it was almost possible to believe that these woeful episodes had been consigned to history. As the most extreme expressions of Christian dogma abated, humanist principles of tolerance and equality arising from the Enlightenment led to emancipation for many European Jews, first as a concept and then codified by the French Revolution, spread throughout the continent by Napoleon and given further impetus with the pan-European revolts of 1848. There followed a period of relative harmony in Jewish-Gentile relations, in western Europe at least.

Everything changed with the Franco-Prussian War of 1870–71, an event within living memory for all of Bahr's respondents, and a turning point which we can take as our baseline for examining early modern antisemitism. Of the two countries most closely considered in the book, it created one (Germany) and was a profound caesura in the other (France) which finally, definitively established the republican model.

In the political sphere the age was marked by the rapid rise of nationalism, which in many cases

ANTISEMITISM

endeavoured to impose hierarchies of citizenry or binary modes of belonging/exclusion onto highly heterogeneous populations, mirroring the work of classification going on in the natural sciences at the time. Modern antisemitism was still in part informed by ancient religious antipathies, but what Bahr's text reflects is an alarming escalation in anti-Jewish sentiment that, crucially, replaced faith with race.

Here we see the emergence of the Jewish 'question' or 'problem', which called for a solution. For the modern antisemite, conversion was not the answer – the Jew was *inherently* malicious, a quality that no amount of holy water could expunge. Assimilation was not the answer – the Jew would merely be going under cover. Cohabitation was not the answer – given a free hand the Jew would come to dominate the majority culture. The late 19th century gave rise to a number of antisemitic tropes that persist to this day: the association of Jews with the excesses of free market capitalism, conspiracy theories that divined the hand of Jewish cabals in all manner of unscrupulous dealings, along with specific traits such as guile and duplicity.

In an age of widespread financial speculation and rapidly acquired fortunes, there was equally widespread suspicion of wealth gained not through labour or inheritance but investment, a phenomenon associated in the public imagination with Jews in particular. The 'blood-sucking' Jew of medieval legend – the avaricious money-lender, but also the parasite literally killing Christians for ritual purposes in the most extreme anti-Jewish legends – had now turned his attention to capital markets and would, the theory went, bleed them and their host nations dry. These notions were freely aligned with a wide variety of other political ideas of the time in ways that can surprise the present-day reader; anti-Jewish feeling was by no means confined to the reactionary right wing.

This brings us to a crucial point that helps explain why antisemitism could attain such heinous intensity – it was an extremely adaptable prejudice that could assume religious, racial, social, economic, political or cultural dimensions as required. Like a grappling hook, its strength and tenacity increased exponentially when two or more prongs were activated simultaneously. For the beneficiaries of declining economic structures, Jewry could be fashioned to represent the new power of capital, but the ethnicity of figures like Karl Marx and Ferdinand Lassalle also meant that socialism could be characterised as a Jewish conspiracy. Jews could subvert from above or below, as the covert string-pullers of international finance or as bedraggled immigrants from distant shtetls, competing in the market for low-paid labour. An early 20th-century German postcard neatly illustrates this duality in paired caricatures, with a Jewish hawker in ringlets selling coin purses alongside a big-nosed, cigar-smoking plutocrat counting his piles of gold coins.

In Germany, the constitution of the new empire formed in the wake of the Franco-Prussian War in 1871 had enshrined emancipation, imposing it on those recalcitrant German states that had yet to implement it. But there was a wide gulf between de jure and de facto equality; Jews were unofficially barred from leading positions in the military and the public service, the most prestigious fields of endeavour for ambitious young men at the time. In these institutions, and among the Junkers, among the imperial court and other representatives of the old aristocratic order, Jews were viewed with mistrust, disdain and enmity, and Jewish speculators were blamed for the sharp economic downturn that marred the first few years of the empire.

Adolf Stoecker epitomised the transition from religious to racial antisemitism. The court chaplain to the first Kaiser, Wilhelm I, he used his eminent position to spread his extreme anti-Jewish views, which held that the biblical, religious guilt of the Jews resulted from a genetic disposition to evil. Stoecker drew from Luther – reminding us that religious antisemitism was by no means solely a Catholic phenomenon – but took his teachings well beyond the pulpit. In 1878 he formed the Christian Social Workers' Party which combined some light anti-capitalism with more reactionary views and, in particular, antisemitism, making it one of the first political organisations to incorporate hatred of Jews as a central plank in its platform.

Wilhelm Marr, meanwhile, exemplified the era's strange new ideological amalgams. Both an anarchist and an atheist, in 1879 Marr produced two pamphlets that held 'Germanism' and Judaism to be implacable adversaries, advising/warning how either might ultimately win/lose against the other. He is credited with bringing the term *Antisemitismus* into popular usage, and also founded a short-lived 'League of Antisemites'. He was a key figure in the 'Antisemitism Dispute' (1879–1881) that also pitted historians Heinrich von Treitschke and Theodor Mommsen against each other, during which Treitschke claimed that 'the Jews are our misfortune', a phrase later adopted by the Nazis.

The 1880s brought anti-Jewish conferences and a publishing boom of journals and books dealing with the issue for which Eugen Dühring's *The Jewish Question as a Question of Race, Customs and Culture* (1881) may stand as representative. Often wrapped in pseudo-science, presenting unfounded sociological assertion as inarguable fact, they sometimes proposed violent 'solutions' which the era's otherwise vigilant censors chose to overlook. Wilhelm II, who came to the throne in 1888, was unquestionably an antisemite even if he kept his public utterances on the matter to a minimum. In 1893, German political antisemitism achieved its greatest gains prior to the rise of the Nazis when two parties trading largely in hatred of Jews together won 18 seats in the Reichstag. The most contentious of their number was Hermann Ahlwardt, an inarticulate rabble-rouser who whipped up controversies that invariably had a Jewish component, such as the *Judenflinte* ('Jew Guns') scandal.

France, like Germany, underwent enormous upheavals after the Franco-Prussian War. The first half of the Third Republic which was forged in the conflict saw a wide range of journals and books targeting Jewish influence in society. The most visible organ of traditional, Catholic antisemitism in modern vestments was *La Croix*, a newspaper founded in 1883. Anti-Jewish feeling attained particular momentum with the 1886 publication of *La*

France Juive (Jewish France), an extensive and hugely popular work which combined religious, economic and racial antisemitism, with now-familiar targets such as the Rothschild family. Its author was Édouard Drumont, assisted by two of Bahr's interviewees, Alphonse Daudet and Francis Magnard. Within a few years Drumont had formed the Antisemitic League of France and launched the anti-Jewish daily newspaper *La Libre Parole*. But he was far from the only public figure exploiting the appeal of antisemitism.

The Franco-Prussian war had deprived France of Alsace, with its significant Jewish minority, including a certain Captain Dreyfus whose wrongful arrest would soon trigger a scandal that would expose the depth of antisemitism in the country. While greatly overshadowed by the Dreyfus Affair today, the earlier Panama Scandal was still sending shock waves through France at the time of Bahr's book, and its impact at the time is difficult to overestimate, not least the antisemitic dimension to the accusations that attended it. It arose after the collapse of the first large-scale attempt to construct a canal through Panama, a disastrous project in which France invested – and lost – vast sums. While work stopped in 1889, the economic aftershocks were felt for years, revealing large-scale corruption that ran through the political, financial and industrial spheres. Two figures in this affair aroused particular hostility, being of German-Jewish origin, and thus doubly suspect – Cornelius Herz and Baron Jacques Reinach.

This concentration on Germany and France, which together account for over three-quarters of Bahr's book, should not suggest that the rest of Europe was untroubled by antisemitism, merely that these two countries were the centres of a new *politicised* strain of anti-Jewish sentiment. There were certainly stirrings in Bahr's homeland, despite the imperial regime's relatively benign attitude to Jews and other minorities in the huge, multi-ethnic Austro-Hungarian conglomerate, and the numerous Jewish exponents of the flourishing Viennese avant-garde of the time. The pan-German movement, which advocated a confederation that would sever Austria from its eastern vassal states and append it to the German Empire, was not necessarily anti-Jewish to begin with but became so in the 1880s under the influence of Georg von Schönerer, who would exert an enormous influence on 20th-century antisemitism. Elsewhere in the empire, Hungarian politician Győző Istóczy established a 'Non-Jewish Federation' in 1880. And further east conditions were worse still. The Russian Empire, untouched by the wave of emancipation in the rest of Europe, witnessed devastating pogroms throughout the 1880s which led to large-scale westward emigration of its Jewish subjects.

We owe it to the progressive figures of this time to note that prominent voices spoke out against this new antisemitism, and like their adversaries they inhabited a spectrum of diverse, even contradictory views. Author Émile Zola, for instance, was loudly opposed to prejudice even before the Dreyfus Affair and his seismic 'J'accuse…!' article. Theodor Mommsen campaigned vigorously against antisemitism and in 1886, Friedrich Nietzsche famously broke with Richard Wagner because of the latter's extreme antisemitic views.

The foregoing certainly suggests why someone might have wished to undertake a serious study of antisemitism in 1893. What it doesn't explain is why that someone should be an Austrian writer best known at the time as a theatre critic.

Hermann Bahr's back story rewards examination, not just because he is a compelling figure whose outstanding contribution to the artistic and literary tumult of fin-de-siècle Vienna, pan-European culture and the advance of Modernism in general has barely been acknowledged in English-language texts. What we will also discover is that – through his studies, his associates, his preoccupations, his shifting cultural identity, his intellectual development – he was in fact prodigiously well positioned to offer a panoramic survey of European antisemitism in his time; not least because he himself had journeyed through much of the continuum of opinions occupied by his respondents.

Born in solidly middle-class, typically Catholic circumstances in Linz in 1863, Hermann Bahr early on exhibited a sharp mind and a rebellious spirit; graduating from secondary school as a star pupil in 1881, he was allowed to address his fellow students and caused a stir by using his talk to champion socialism. At university in Vienna, where he studied classical philology and philosophy, Bahr became an associate member of Albia, a *Burschenschaft* (a student association comparable to a fraternity) which was aligned with the pan-German movement. It was here that he came into contact with two figures who dramatically exemplified the range of responses to the 'Jewish question' at the time. On the one hand there was Theodor Herzl, the first modern Zionist, one of a number of Jews at the time who, with no previous cause to regard themselves as significantly other, responded to anti-Jewish agitation with increased identification with Judaism. On the other was Georg von Schönerer, the early instigator of racial antisemitism who would exert an enormous ideological influence on Nazism. Here, Bahr had personal links with the respective godfathers of modern Israel and the Holocaust.

To Bahr's later shame, it was Schönerer who loomed largest in his thinking at the time. The passionate young pan-Germanist could see at close quarters those qualities he admired from afar in Otto von Bismarck, Richard Wagner and Friedrich Nietzsche. Adopting Schönerer's views as his own, Bahr saw the Austro-Hungarian Empire as an 'over-Slavified' relic of the past. One of Bahr's first published articles reflected his antisemitic beliefs, which found even cruder expression in slogans that he pasted up around Vienna, leading to his arrest.

In 1883 Bahr aired his outspoken pan-German views at a ceremony to mark the death of Richard Wagner and was dismissed from Vienna University for 'treasonous activities'; he then moved to Graz, where he was arrested for insulting Jewish patrons in a café. It was an ignominious nadir. The worldly man of letters was yet to emerge, and in the meantime Bahr pursued sociology and economics, a combination of disciplines he regarded as the 'alchemy of the future'. So when he moved to Berlin in 1884 it was as much the presence of famed economists Adolph Wagner and Gustav Schmoller as his

Germanophilia that attracted him.

Hermann Bahr arrived in Berlin with a highly quixotic blend of political beliefs, favouring a Hohenzollern monarchy ruling over Germany and Austria (but not the rest of Austria's empire), free of Jewish influence and somehow also socialist. His admiration for Bismarck led Bahr to join a torchlight procession for the Iron Chancellor's 70th birthday in 1885. He endeavoured to meet the man himself but was directed instead to an advisor, Franz Johannes von Rottenburg, who inspired an unexpected turning point. Rottenburg managed to convince the committed pan-Germanist of the necessity of Austrian sovereignty; Bahr became an Austrian patriot on the spot – and would remain so for the rest of his life – even as his antisemitic and socialist views receded.

From this transitional phase a writer was emerging. *Die neuen Menschen* (The New People), from 1887, was emblematic of Bahr's shifting focus. Thematically it illustrated his gradual alienation from socialism but its form – drama – would increasingly come to preoccupy him as both a critic and a creator. The following year he met the foremost living practitioner of the art, Henrik Ibsen, and moved to Paris where he could satisfy his hunger for new literary forms.

Bahr dwelt among bohemians and came into contact with Decadent literature, with the key text of the movement, Joris-Karl Huysmans's *À rebours,* inspiring his first novel, *Die gute Schule* (The Good School, 1890). He was one of the first German-speaking writers to regard the radical individualism and recherché perversity of Decadence as a way forward, as reflected in one of his most renowned essays, 'Die Überwindung des Naturalismus' (Overcoming Naturalism) in 1891.

As well as travelling to Spain, Morocco and Russia, Bahr returned to Berlin, where he was repelled by the advance of materialism, and in marked contrast to his younger years came to regard Jews as guardians of German culture (although he also complained that Germans were 'two hundred years behind' when he worked on the journal *Freie Bühne für modernes Leben*, or Free Stage for Modern Life). Through his literary criticism Bahr became closely identified in German-speaking Europe with *die Moderne* and he played a crucial role in the advancement of new forms.

Amid an intense period of publishing activity, Bahr issued a collection of stories entitled *Fin de Siècle*, helping to popularise a French borrowing that would come to be used as an umbrella term in German-speaking countries for Decadence, Symbolism and other inter-connected literary strains at the close of the 19th century. However, six of the book's tales were judged obscene by Prussian authorities for depicting 'abnormal and aberrant gratification of the sex drive', and Bahr was fined 150 marks.

In 1891 Bahr returned to Vienna, with no little reluctance initially, although he soon became an essential part of the city's literary life at one of its most exciting periods. Again, Bahr was pivotal, the ringleader of the 'Young Vienna' group which included the likes of Arthur Schnitzler, Stefan Zweig and Hugo von Hofmannsthal, as well as Karl Kraus, with whom Bahr conducted a long-running feud. In 1892 Bahr met Emil

Auspitzer, the Jewish editor of Vienna's *Deutsche Zeitung*, a newspaper that went through a number of ideological shifts. Auspitzer took Bahr on with a handsome salary and a generous brief that encompassed theatre as well as wider cultural phenomena, and Bahr made the most of it. In October of that year he ran a series of interviews with notable figures in Vienna's theatre scene. This was a highly novel concept in German-language letters; the authoritative Duden dictionary locates the first instance of the loan word *das Interview* in 1887. Toward the end of that year Bahr returned to Paris to cover the Panama Scandal, interviewing Émile Zola among others, and also met up with Theodor Herzl again, who was there covering the same story as the foreign correspondent for the *Neue Freie Presse*, competitor to the *Deutsche Zeitung*.

In 1893 Bahr marshalled these elements for a far more extensive undertaking – a series of interviews with prominent international figures on the subject of antisemitism. He was quite open about the model for the project: *Enquête sur l'évolution littéraire* (Enquiry into Literary Evolution) by French journalist Jules Huret, a series published in the newspaper *L'Écho de Paris* in 1891, and issued as a book in the same year. Zola, Verlaine, Maupassant, Huysmans and many others – Huret's study of contemporary literary currents included a truly remarkable selection of *hommes des lettres* (and just one *femme*, author Juliette Adam). It was not just his interviewees' forthright views that he captured, but also their personalities, their sensibilities, their surroundings.

The following year a certain Curt Grottewitz

attempted something similar for German literature, although he solicited responses by mail for his study. On its release Bahr discussed both this and Huret's book; his contempt for the German (perhaps mingled with envy for a man who had trumped his idea) was matched only by his admiration for Huret, and his contrast of the two offers us an insight into his own priorities which can be considered programmatic for his own imminent engagement with the form:

> The Frenchman visited each artist
> and drew out the secret nature of each; not what
> they said to him, but how he viewed them and
> gleaned from quiet signs, from the arrangement
> of the furniture, from the careless manner of
> greeting, from a casual gesture, from the whole
> air of glances and tones, and surprised each
> in his nightshirt, so to speak – that is the merit
> of his writing. The German simply sent them
> a survey with a few questions and there each wrote
> his opinion which we have long known anyway
> and we do not discover anything new. That is the
> difference between art and craft.

'But,' he adds, unable to resist a final barb, 'even as craft the book is not up to much.' Looking back on Huret ten years later, Bahr described the interview format in customarily combative terms: 'The interview, in fact, is a conflict between two people on a certain question in the form of a polite conversation, about who is the stronger; intellectual fencing or boxing in which the journalist seeks to confuse, numb and exhaust so that in the end his opponent loses his footing, his pose and his self-consciousness and reveals himself.'

The innovations that Bahr introduced as he adopted this model were to expand the geographical scope of his enquiries and, in contrast to the rather rarefied discourse of litterateurs, use them to address an issue that affected all of society. On 25 March 1893 he announced to readers of the *Deutsche Zeitung*: 'Once again I am venturing out into the world to find out what people are thinking and saying.' In his prefatory remarks he spends no time considering the origins of antisemitism or how it had developed over time, rather he opens with the bald assertion that it is a pathology, or addiction, and concentrates on the feeling it evokes. Intriguingly, Bahr does not ask his respondents to comment on the status of Jews in society, but on *antisemitism*. This offered some interviewees the opportunity to express modish disapproval for a current political phenomenon while ignoring their own unexamined prejudices.

From the interview that follows his introduction, conducted with the author Friedrich Spielhagen in Berlin, it is clear that he has taken Huret's approach to heart. Bahr evokes a sense of time and place, describing a lived encounter with a real person in a physical space rather than a mere airing of notions. Eager though he is to make us aware of who and what he knows, there is also a generosity in his descriptions, an intimacy which he invites us to share. There is a strong sense that we, through our intermediary Bahr, are catching these grandees, scribes and public intellectuals off-guard.

The series continued throughout 1893, with each article beginning at the bottom of the front page, a position many German-language newspapers of the time reserved for the *Feuilleton*, a looser, more personal interpretation of contemporary life than the news articles above it. By summer Bahr was finished with his German subjects, with all but Ernst Haeckel interviewed in Berlin, and had moved on to Paris, where he also met two prominent Spanish exiles. In high summer his English and Irish interviewees were corralled into one long article and before the coming of autumn he had proceeded through Belgium and arrived at Norway (on paper at least).

You could argue that Bahr was tracing antisemitism from its centre at the time (Berlin), following a route of diminishing intensity to arrive at the site of least impact (Scandinavia). We may consider it a source of regret that Bahr did not interview any of his compatriots; the inclusion of one of the numerous Jewish representatives of 'Young Vienna', not to mention other perspectives from an empire with a significant Jewish minority, might have contributed greatly to a pan-European perspective of antisemitism. An interview with Bahr's friend Theodor Herzl, for instance, would have provided a fascinating insight into the development of Zionism as a response to antipathy toward Jews, especially in central and eastern Europe. But these idle wishes seem churlish when you consider the hugely valuable document that actually resulted.

It is impossible not to ponder Bahr's methods. Was he transcribing the extensive passages of direct speech as he went? Or did he recall them afterwards?

Certainly his experience as a dramatist is apparent – many articles begin with long descriptions of the location, as though establishing the stage set before the characters are permitted to enter and declaim their dialogue. Some interviews were preceded by long preambles while others, especially those grouped together in larger articles, were necessarily more sketch-like. In a few instances Bahr runs through a checklist of his subject's achievements, as was the case with General Cluseret, whose CV reads like an outlandish picaresque novel.

In Bahr, mockery often appeared to proceed from a competitive impulse, a response to those who – like the hapless Grottewitz – had advanced into territory he had staked out for himself. We see this in his introductory description of the more successful journalist Harden, presented in a baroque style that seems to parody the German's own notoriously convoluted syntax. Bahr's unflattering profile of *Le Figaro* editor Francis Magnard claims 'He is always a snob or philistine in a form that others will only assume six months hence', although he would later say of himself, 'I was involved in almost every intellectual fashion, but beforehand, in other words before it became a fashion.' For Charles Morice he channels the mysteries of Symbolist prose, the Frenchman being identified with the movement in a way Bahr never was.

In his visit to the prominent Belle Époque journalist Séverine, an outspoken defender of progressive causes, Bahr carries the scene-setting preamble to an extreme. It alone is as long as most of his other pieces, and it drips with condescension, viewing her considerable achievements entirely through the prism of gender, her outstanding work rate characterised as something akin to witchcraft. There is little to be said in Bahr's defence concerning his attitudes to women, which blended traditional chauvinism with reductive female archetypes drawn from fin-de-siècle literature.

To read these interviews is to undergo sudden and complete immersion in a fast-flowing stream of references and inferences that sweeps us through a large swathe of western Europe. Many of these people, places and events are presented without commentary, as though glossing would break the conspiratorial bond of intimacy and assumed knowledge between writer and reader. Bahr's erudition is never far from the surface. Even before he pitches up in Paris, he is salting his text with untranslated French quotes, peppering it with references to French culture and politics to leave us in no doubt that he is au fait with the concerns of the Parisian chattering classes.

While the words of the interviewees lay out a broad spectrum of opinion in numerous gradations – these are interviews and not multiple-choice surveys, after all – there are identifiable commonalities in their statements, consistent patterns, recurring tropes, shared themes, theories and views which are worth summarising.

A number of interviewees – such as Barth, Mommsen, Foerster and Wentworth – echo Bahr's view of the *irrationality or pathology of antisemitism*, describing it in terms of disease (Mommsen: 'Antisemitism cannot be refuted any more than a disease can be refuted'); Spielhagen, Rickert, Barth, Mackay, Mommsen, Séverine and Zorrilla emphasise the antisemites' immunity to reason or discussion (Rickert: 'Words cannot help against antisemitism') or, like Ibsen, hold antisemitism to be simply beyond comprehension.

There is widespread agreement among both proponents and opponents of antisemitism alike – Spielhagen, Barth, Haeckel, Simon, Leroy-Beaulieu, Meyer, Morice, Cluseret, Rocherfort, Picard – of an *antisemitism devoid of religious sentiment*, or of a religious aspect that is merely a pretext (Rochefort: 'I am a passionate, fanatic antisemite. But I reject all religious antisemitism. It is dumb and stupid'). But Spielhagen, Barth, Bebel, Foerster and others describe it in economic terms, readily *conflating capitalist excesses with Jews*, or – like Wagner, Harden, Whitman, Cluseret and Picard – emphasising the distinction between money 'gained' and 'earned' (Picard: 'Jews, those parasites who only ever enrich themselves without creating anything'). Foerster, who was a member of Mommsen's Association for Defence against Antisemitism, ascribes 'a highly significant share in the distress and suffering' of the poor in central and eastern Europe to Jews and even the Jewish Harden proclaims his opposition to 'the middle-man spirit', 'the stock market mob', 'the putrid egotism of the bourgeoisie', and offers no clear distinction to suggest that these qualities were not necessarily Jewish.

Numerous respondents, on the other hand, draw *distinctions between different groups of Jews*, with frequent disdain for newer Jewish immigrants from the East. This is common to Germany (Schmoller, Wagner, Haeckel), France (Naquet, Leroy-Beaulieu), Britain

(Wentworth, Balfour, Besant, noting the newly settled migrants in London's East End) and Ireland (Healy, referring to the pedlars in his country). Some French interviewees also single out 'German' or Alsatian Jews (Simon, Cluseret, Meyer), while Leroy-Beaulieu contests that it is actually antisemitism that originated on 'the other side of the Rhine'.

Questions of *assimilation and exceptionalism* preoccupy many respondents. Jews stand accused for their otherness, those who assimilate are just as roundly criticised for 'aping' the ways of the majority culture (Picard). Many German-Jewish citizens converted to Protestantism or changed their names; interviewee Maximilian Harden did both, but he also finds Gentile and Jewish Germans 'too similar'. Like Schoenaich-Carolath, Haeckel calls for Jews to 'abandon their peculiarities and completely merge' and even the ponderous, pompous yet ostensibly benign Egidy proves to be a radical assimilationist ('there will be nothing to prevent those people who still call themselves Jews today from combining religiously – and now also racially – with the host peoples whose lands they have inhabited for centuries'). Some interviewees note that antisemitism actually exacerbated differences, as Jews are forced into 'particularity' (Leroy-Beaulieu) or *'mis à part'* (Harden), a view shared by Morice and Naquet. Conversely, in locations with negligible or long-assimilated Jewish populations, such as Spain and Belgium, the distinction between Jews and Gentiles is held to be fluid and inconsequential (Sawa: 'The Castilian is much more foreign to the Andalusian than the Jew is to the Christian'). In light of later legislation in both France and Germany that singled out Jews and formed the 'legal' foundation of the Holocaust, it is worth noting that even the most antisemitic of Bahr's respondents (Cluseret, Rochefort) explicitly reject the idea of specific laws that would target their foes.

Relatively few interviewees take a longer *historical perspective*. Both Spanish respondents lament the expulsion of Jews from their country centuries beforehand; Séverine notes that Jews had been forced into money-lending and other professions for which they were later so derided, while Leroy-Beaulieu points to the impossibility of defining a 'pure' race in Europe with its millennia of intermixing.

A number of respondents ponder the strange *alliances and paradoxes* forged by antisemitism, particularly in France with its unusual bonds between reactionary and revolutionary forces (generally Catholics and socialists) as noted by Leroy-Beaulieu, Simon and Naquet ('a funny old mix'). Haeckel actually regards Jews as allies against Catholic influence in Germany, while Bebel and Simon both feel that letting antisemitism run its course would ultimately benefit socialism (although only Bebel approves of this strategy). Barth sees antisemitism as the 'socialism of the Junkers' while Séverine is bemused by the coalition of aristocrats, socialists and street brawlers united solely by their hatred of Jews.

At the extremes of sentiment there is *philosemitism* (Morice: 'great, rare, indispensable gifts'; Sawa: 'A people that can boast Heine, Marx, Lassalle merits glory and love') balanced by the *naked antisemitism* of Wagner, Rochefort, Cluseret, Daudet and Picard, which is often 'justified' by conspiracy theories (Daudet: 'in all those dirty dealings the Jews always play the leading role – well, ultimately it becomes difficult to avoid a certain antipathy').

Like Édouard Drumont, the figure of Hermann Ahlwardt does not appear in person but is often invoked by others. The German politician is described as a fanatic, able to gain followers for his hateful views without the gift of eloquence, or even coherence. Theodor Barth's assessment is typical: 'He babbles vapidly, a thousand ridiculous things all mixed up together … It is simply a mystery what the masses find in him – except the mean pleasure of slander, defamation and scandal; the mob seeks amusement, and nothing amuses it more than hearing decent people slandered and insulted.' But shortly after the project began Bahr did in fact conduct an interview with Ahlwardt. While it ran in the *Deutsche Zeitung* it was expressly omitted from the *Antisemitism* series, perhaps because the tone is too jarringly unhinged, with Ahlwardt presenting as a raving, delusional grotesque. 'I am radical, I am far more radical, I am the most radical, and that's why all the nations of Europe follow me, they'll all follow me, all of them, all of them – the petty differences between Germany and the French or Russians must be stilled, they don't mean anything; everyone must join forces, all of Europe, against the Jews, against the Jews – I have no mercy any more, just as they had no mercy with me, no mercy!' Ahlwardt was at least lucid enough to be horrified by the resulting article, and claimed that it was invented, that he had exchanged nothing more than pleasantries with Bahr before showing him the door. Bahr countered with numerous details of their meeting, claiming in fact that it was he who had tried to take his leave, that the discussion with Ahlwardt wasn't worth 'the cost of my waiting coach'. 'In my interview there is not a word that Mr Ahlwardt did not utter,' summarised Bahr, 'but in fact Mr Ahlwardt uttered much that is not in my interview; I owe this consideration to my readers' nerves and to common decency.'

Surely one of the most dispiriting elements for a present-day reader is how persistent these methods of hatred and fomentation, these irrational appeals to bigotry have been. We may also note how some elements of the media were willing to use provocation and division as a conscious strategy for increasing revenue, like the newspaper that 'gained three thousand subscribers in the last quarter with antisemitic agitation' (Barth). Naturally there is dramatic irony aplenty, and while it would be unjust to confront figures of the past with their lack of clairvoyance, nor can we ignore the stark lesson from history provided by the numerous respondents who claimed that if left to its own devices, antisemitism would soon exhaust itself.

Bahr's very approach – and remember this was a time of accelerating nationalist belligerence – suggests that antisemitism was a *European* problem requiring a *European* solution, a sweeping scope that renders his series far more than just a series of interviews. A decade later he was referring hopefully to a 'United States of Europe', and appeared to aspire to a community of commonality of even more extensive dimensions: 'These people of great desire scattered throughout the world, who feel the same, hope the same, fear the same as we do, they are the true fatherland.'

Within this expansive vision Bahr is receptive to the small details that lend substance and vitality to his reports, acute observations such as August Bebel's 'exhaustion and pallor' which is 'caused less by great turns of fate than small daily sorrows', 'the embers of Granada' in the eyes of Alejandro Sawa or the irreverent comparison of Tim Healy with a 'nimble little lizard'. He has a great gift for evoking speech, such as that of Gustav Schmoller, 'gliding as though slipper-shod', or Jules Simon's which 'begins in shrill tones then falls breathlessly and extinguishes in darkness', or the telegraph-like concision of Francis Magnard, whose interlocutor is 'left to establish the conjunctions'.

One of the rich pleasures of this book is that an attentive commentator like Bahr also encounters so many things in passing, fragmentary images that have little to do with the matter at hand, but which fuse to plot a vista of the age – something between a kaleidoscope and a panorama. From the busy corridors of power to the quiet, well-scrubbed staircases of outlying apartment buildings, he notes the order or the disarray in which his interviewees dwell, the busts and etchings with which they people their solitude. There are the transitional moments of history, such as the ruins of the Cour des Comptes burned down in the Commune which have still not been taken away to be replaced by the Gare (now Musée) d'Orsay. The arcane, archaic twists of the Spanish succession, which seem to issue from a 17th-century drama, are treated as matters of pressing currency.

There are strong traces of anarchy and other strategies of liberation that were afoot at the time, as well as the late 19th-century spiritual revival. A return to robust dogmatic foundations is contrasted with the esoteric innovations of Madame Blavatsky, or the more recondite mysticism of the Symbolists and Decadents. Bahr evokes fin-de-siècle motifs – faith as 'chloral', a 'congenial anaesthetic that gives one strange dreams' amid an era of 'subtle, rare, carefully curated sensations' – and name-checks their proponents, such as Paul Verlaine, Ola Hansson and Rachilde.

Visiting an early multimedia platform at Parisian newspaper *Le Gaulois*, Bahr witnesses the vaulting ambition of information commerce that would result in today's data behemoths: 'But here they seek to take care of all his business, all his concerns, to facilitate every desire. They wish to become assistants in the life of the reader. They wish to manage everything for him. Their aim is that he should seek advice and assistance from them for every question, every quandary, every need.'

The *Antisemitism* series concluded in September 1893 with the three Belgian interviewees, appended with the curt response from Bjørnstjerne Bjørnson. The project both attested to and furthered Bahr's extraordinary cultural reach. Shortly after the series came to an end, Bahr announced in the *Deutsche Zeitung*, with some justification if not modesty, that 'between the Volga and the Loire, from the Thames to the Guadalquivir there is nothing felt that I cannot comprehend, share and shape … the European soul has no secrets from me.'

Antisemitism was issued as a book in late 1894 by S. Fischer, a publishing house then in its infancy which is now a giant of the German book trade. The edition dropped one interview (in the form of a letter) with Rudolf von Gneist, a German jurist, politician and member of the Association for Defence against Antisemitism, while it gained the interview with the outspoken Henri Rochefort which had not previously been published.

To suggest that Hermann Bahr the young rowdy and unthinking conduit of antisemitic abuse one day saw the light and thereafter strode forth as a steadfast ally of Jewry and enemy of prejudice is a little simplistic but broadly correct in outline. Little could better illustrate the journey Bahr had undertaken from the bigotry of his student days than his 1895 marriage to Rosa Jokl, a Jewish actress.

Meanwhile antisemitism had not 'exhausted' itself as some of Bahr's respondents had predicted, or hoped. A number of interviewees both French and foreign would take sides in the Dreyfus Affair which was just breaking as the book went to press, as Alfred Dreyfus, an Alsatian Jew and captain in the French army, was wrongly convicted of treason in December 1894. The case would drag on for years, bringing profound division to France. While German political antisemitism had passed its pre-Nazi peak, it was merely resting, and in Bahr's own home of Vienna the mayor Karl Lueger was modelling a form of populist antisemitism that later attracted the admiration of Adolf Hitler.

Bahr continued to publish, although his steady flow of dramas ceased around the start of the First World

War. His 1916 essay 'Expressionismus' showed that he still had an appreciation for the latest literary modes, but this would soon abate, and the works of his later years were instead devoted to Catholicism and Austrian patriotism. A long-running column in the *Neues Wiener Journal* at least kept him in the minds of readers who may have ceased buying his books, although he continued to publish, with 1919 bringing *Die Rotte Korahs*, a novel that represented his most intense engagement with Judaism in fiction. In 1922 he and his second wife, Wagnerian soprano Anna von Mildenburg, moved to Munich, and Bahr spent the rest of his life there. Hermann Bahr died in 1934, outliving all of his interviewees and surviving just long enough to witness the rise of the Third Reich, the reality of which would outstrip the direst predictions of the most pessimistic among them.